The Last Muse

The Last Muse

Ian McMaster

THE LAST MUSE

Copyright © 2019, Ian McMaster.

All rights reserved. No part of this publication may be reproduced, stored in a retrieval system, or transmitted in any form or by any means, electronic, mechanical, photocopying, recording, or otherwise, without written permission of the author and publisher.

Published by Poetry for Change, Edmonton, Canada

ISBN
PAPERBACK: 978-1-77354-294-2
EBOOK: 978-1-77354-295-9

Dedicated to my mother and daughters

Introduction

I find it odd that I have arrived here. With such timing. This should not have been the preface for everything to come. I began writing at a very young age and put it to the side. Like so many others in the world, I ignored a passion for a reason, a season and a life time.

A crossroad had presented itself a few years ago and I walked away from everything I had always been told. I had been pretending all along, fooling myself and others. Had I stumbled across myself sooner, perhaps all the heartache, shattered promises and broken worlds would have been avoided. After all. I had it all, right? The wife, the great kids, the house, the cars. What I really had were demons of days gone before. And they whispered, oh, how they whispered endlessly. Coupled with anothers, they ran rampant through our lives, intertwined. I had always felt the pull inside me, I chose to ignore it.

For all the knowledge and wisdom imparted upon me from those who came before, had told me otherwise. I lied to myself with venomous intent. I do not believe anything would have changed however, I would have stayed the course. I gave up the ones who should have been my muses forever more, for I could not see the light in the darkness of my sheltered woods. I failed myself and I failed my family. For I had people to impress, people that never mattered. Not truly anyway, not at the end of the day.

Looking back on it all, one could say, at least I found my true self. And they would be correct, on one level. But now, the days grow short. In a way, my apologies are all to come, in one form or another. So I hope those who deserve them the most may read them here. For they are here, in all their glory. Hidden, like I from the world, a world I do not belong to.

I originally had a lot more to say about all the years that came before this book but have decided to leave the past back on those pages. It most certainly will creep through in the words that lay ahead. So here I sit, at my table....typing feverishly as the words flow. Before they become as lost to me as I have to myself. For you see, I no longer know if my reality has become the illusion or if the delusions have become my reality. I may have dove too deep lately. They always said there is a fine line between creativity and madness, and a chance that I may have crossed it. If that is my fate, then so be it. It's a fairly blissful state, I cannot see a reason to stray back for too long.

I walk alone now, by choice. I try and make amends as I go, for my children. However, I never get out of my head long enough to fully realize that it is just as easy to succeed with them as it is to fail. So I stumble, time and time again. Every time I feel like I finally have a foothold to climb out from the abyss of my own mind, I pull myself once more from that ledge. I hope one day they will understand that it was never them. They were just trying to be loved by a man who cannot love, not like they know it to be. I do love, you know, it is just my own twisted version of it.

The irony is now, that I have found my own personal truths. In all their glory, I see them through all the clouds and light. And like a person strolling through an antique store, I pick them up. I handle them carefully, appreciate their uniqueness and beauty. I see my happiness in their reflections. The path to sharing myself once more with others has never been so clear of debris. I see just how simple it could be. How natural it would feel. And then, then I set them back down and head for the door. Like I have always done. The difference now is, I know. So I never have to flip the open for business sign on my heart again and fool another into stepping through the entrance into nothing but a void.

You see, the antiques that lay inside me are just projections. Ideas of a person I should be, a human I could be. Perhaps a man that I used to be. Which of those, is never certain. Instead, what I have now are words. Words that steady my head, hold my soul in place for a time. And muses, oh the muses of my life. They came in so many forms. To finally free my words from the bonds I place on them. The ideas always swirling, forming but never coming to fruition. Without my muses, I would have had nothing.

Now however, I no longer dream of possession of these most beautiful creatures. I see me, I see them. I see what they offer to the world and I understand that I must never reach beyond my means. So I watch over them, from afar. Love is now a simple appreciation for another human spirit that allows me to walk beside them for a time. Every single interaction has been treasured, locked away in a place that will accompany me as I walk off into the nether. I will never stay put, I will never hold fast. I am but a hopeless man, wandering the depths of his sanity that is rather insane.

So, I thank you. With all the heart I can give. The muses, who inspire people to create. Whether it be me or someone else. In painting, poetry, song, sculpture, novels. However it presents itself. Just know that without you, all the beginnings could never have become endings. In these books, you will find a variety of reasons these pages exist. I hope you may distinguish for yourselves the differences I have written into my words. For most of these people were never ones I desired personally to be held in the prison of me. I will see you beautiful souls on the streets. To most of you, I will turn my eyes to the ground. To some of you, a fire will ignite for a moment. Sit back, light a candle or whatever it is your heart desires and let me tell you a tale. The tale of a man found, lost, confused and found again. I leave you now. With a list of the muses, others involved in their own way and the music that all helped bring forth the gibberish I am about to unleash on you. In no particular order of course, because that would not be me, if I left you with an easy way to decipher my mind. I hope you enjoy the read and if it seems to help in any small way, then perhaps I finally accomplished something all the way through, properly.

Thank You

To my girls, to my family, to the muses of my life; I thank you deeply for everything.

You reached into my soul and stirred a fire in me, a fire that warmed me in the cold. That made me want to rise once more and face the day. You'll never know what it all meant to me, for that is my way. This is but a token, it will get you a boarding pass into my brain. Pay attention for here we lay, pieces of all of us, brought together to make something beautiful. Something intangible, but I tried to capture it anyway.

Lilli, Emma, and Annie....Oh how you make my heart happy, watching you grow into wonderful young women. It was never by my hand and believe me, that is one thing I would most certainly change if I could. I would want my time back with you. I never showed you what it meant to be a good father, a good dad or a good husband to your mother. Well, perhaps there were glimpses of brilliance in my foolishness but never enough. Going forward however, as you are growing too fast to go back, perhaps I can show you instead what it means to be a good human.

Amanda....Hmmm, all the possibilities, if only we had known how to love each other. We had some good times, no? So many good ones. So many bad moments that just slowly kept ripping us further apart. I am truly sorry, for it was far too many years of a terrible imprint we left on each other. But I would not go back. We are here now, and we have these amazing little humans around us. I hope you find my words healing in a way. They helped me. You will forever remain the largest part of my life, through it all. I wish nothing but for you to be good, truly good. You are worthy of a real love, it shall find you and it will be glorious.

Anne And Melanie.... I'm so happy for my two sisters, they found what it truly meant to be happy in their lives. How to share of themselves and hold on to themselves in the same moments. Instead of losing themselves to another, they are now celebrated in anothers love. Thank you to Mike and George for being stand up men and showing them what it truly means to be loved.

Melissa....Dearest Melissa. None of this would really even be happening right now if it was not for you. You came into my life at the exact right moment. There are not even really words for how thankful I am for you. You kept me focused on this goal when I started to wander within myself. So many more amazing memories to come. Besties for life! Even when you are more an asshole than a lady! I did not share your beauty in this book, I felt a little greedy. Sorry, not sorry.

Paige....Ah Paige. A couple of slow days on location, a few texts and it all began. The first muse aside from what already existed in my world. The start of something much larger than I. That beautiful heart of yours, that keeps breaking. One day girlie, that wandering spirit will walk you right into it. There shall be no more heartbreak and you will never find yourself bowed under anothers weight again.

Charlotte...Heh, what can one really say? What has it been? 30 years of flirting? You driving my exes nuts with your antics. Always made me feel special and smile though. The untouchable always has a crazy energy around it. Thank you for all the time you spent lifting my pride and ego off the floor. You will be amazing one day soon, embrace and balance young lady!

Lacy...What an odd way to meet a muse huh? We had nothing but a few cab rides together. Me taking you to see your man, a few chats and I found out you drew some beautiful work. From there it was easy, thank you so much for all the pictures! I hope your life brings you everything that hides within those pieces of work!

Cecilia....Beautiful Cecilia. You were the very last attempt at love in the sense that I understood it. The confines of a relationship that I can never wear again, I tried one last time with you. Oh my, the conversations we had. Your love, so true, found me in a dark place and lit a path. I will forever be thankful even though I could not return the favour and love you properly. Not like that. I shall carry a love for you always though. Because even though we tainted it a bit with notions we did not fully understand, I doubt we ever poisoned each others well enough. The beautiful gypsy, fly free girl. I wish nothing but great things!

Kelly...That smile, it shows the hints of what is to come for you girlie. Be the beacon you need young lady. So much hope, so much drive. So much strength. Your resolve will not be broken and I hope I can find a little more time for you going forth so that you will find your way home to yourself. Thank you for your honesty along the way. With yourself and I.

Aurora...Oh my. Where would I even begin with you? I asked the universe for my last muse. The one who would inspire a thousand poems, not just one or ten. And it was always under the premise of some grand romantic notion. And there you stood, before me. I almost walked away for I did not see. You made me take notice. Thank you! For without it all, I would not have seen that the last muse, was the one to finish the journey that Melissa helped start within me. Trust me when I say, I will nurture that tree even though I will not sit under its shade. Everything makes so much more sense since you have arrived. And when I wander, because I will, it is your choice to remind me....or not. I will do my best to remind myself as well. My heart beats with a new energy now. I have things to do! A life to save and it's finally not anothers but my own. I cannot wait to see you fly on the wings you still have! No need to grow new ones.

And all the other lovely ladies who have graced my life along the way! We may not talk much, some of you not at all. But you still reached out and touched a life. I will carry the memories with a warm smile till the end! Jennifer, Lenora, Karisa, Helena, Hip Girl and so many more.

Here's to the memories still to be made. The places to explore within and outside of ourselves. If I drank more, I would tip a glass right in this moment to you.....but alas! Perhaps another day! When this book is done. We shall all meet and celebrate a little life together. For a time, for a moment! Remember, life and love are the two easiest things we have, it is us that makes them difficult. Let go people, fall backwards off that cliff into the sea that scares us so! We will never cease to amaze ourselves if we do!

Music

Now, for the music. Oh the music that I listened to along the way. I will not get into the thousands of songs that have helped create, inspire. The ones that brought tears and smiles and washed away fears. But I wish to share some of it with you. Maybe they are things you have never heard, chances are with me though I have spammed you with links along the way. Take a listen if you like, this is another one of lifes simplest treasures. The song and dance within our hearts, our heads and these silly little meat sacks we wear.

Dance and sing people, you can never go wrong. Stop that car on the side of the road, get out and crank it! Grab that person, shake them to their soul!

Creep - Who cares? They're all amazing versions of the one song that always speaks to me!

Hallelujah - Who cares? Pick a version! Hah, this song is amazing!

3 Doors Down - When I'm Gone
4 Non Blondes - What's Up
A Perfect Circle - So Long and Thanks for All the Fish
AC/DC - Ride On
Amy Macdonald - This is the Life
Amy Winehouse - Back to Black
Audioslave - Doesn't Remind Me
Billy Currington - People are Crazy
Billy Idol - Rebel Yell
Black Crowes - She Talks to Angels

Blue Rodeo - Bad Timing
Calum Scott - Dancing on My Own
Cam - Burning House
Chris Isaak - Wicked Game
Cornershop - Brimful of Asha
Dire Straits - Walk of Life
Disturbed - The Sound of Silence
Ed Sheeran - Perfect Symphony
Eddie Vedder - Society (hah! see ya when I get a van!)
Eva Cassidy - Tall Trees in Georgia
Foo Fighters - Best of You
Garth Brooks - The Dance
Goo Goo Dolls - Iris
Great White - House of Broken Love
Guns and Roses - Estranged
Hootie and the Blowfish - Let Her Cry
Jon Henrik - Daniels Joik
July Talk - Let Her Know
Kodaline - All I Want
Led Zeppelin - Stairway to Heaven
Leonard Cohen - Waiting for the miracle
Luka Rossi - Hello(Cover)
Metallica - Fade to Black
Mumford and Sons - Wilder Mind
Mumford and Sons - Hopeless Wanderer
Olly Murs - Dance with Me Tonight
Olly Murs - Heart Skips a Beat
Our lady Peace - Pick one I guess...lol
Pantera - Cemetery Gates
Pantera - Hollow
Pantera - This Love
Passenger - Let Her Go
Pharrel Williams - Happy
Plain White T's - Hey There Delilah

Queens of the Stone Age - No-One Knows
Sara Bareilles - Once Upon Another Time
Sara Bareilles - Send Me The Moon
Sara Bareilles - She Used To Be Mine
Sarah McLachlan - Fallen
Sarah Simmons - The Story
Seafret - Oceans
Shinedown - Save Me
Shinedown - Simple Man
Sleeping at Last - Uneven Odds
Staind - It's Been Awhile
The Calling - Wherever You Will Go
The Cult - Fire Woman
The Cure - Friday I'm in Love
The Cure - Lovesong
The Lumineers - Nobody Knows
The Rolling Stones - Paint it Black
The Rolling Stones - Sympathy for the Devil
The Tragically Hip - Pick any! but Wheat Kings is amazinggg
Three Days Grace - I Hate Everything About You
Tool - Yep, any again! but H, Eulogy and 46&2 speak to me
UB40 - Red Red Wine. I mean, come on…dance!
Volbeat - Fallen
Xavier Rudd - Breeze
Xavier Rudd - Spirit Bird

There are just so many more but these have been played a fair bit :)

STORY 1

It's that time of year again mama
The time where the world goes silent
I shut it all out, all the pain
I scream it out, in silence
I'm so sorry mama, never did you right
Lost my way to the man you raised
But I'm home now, I came home
To find your heart still beating
Within myself, within us all
And I won't let you down mama
It's time to become a man
A man you can be proud of

STORY 2

The anguish, will be masked
You'll never see behind
The eyes, they darken
To hide, and abide my will
Instead, smile they shall
As if nothing had ever
Come to pass, come too near
For it is my own heart
And not yours I fear

STORY 3

In the darkness I rise

Born in fires of desire

You wished for me

Asked a universe

Or a god, you see

And now I am arrived

You balk and retreat

For you dare not

See the gifts I bear

Bring them to the world

For all of man to share

STORY 4

As the second tear fell

I wrapped myself in it

The warmth cradled me,

As I sang a song of change

Mind and heart felt ease

For here my most dear,

Is where we belong

STORY 5

It was not I

I interjected

For it was you

Who brought

It down

But then I saw

That you were I

And I was you

And who is he

But he, for you

And before I knew

That hidden glue

Came undone

Before he grew

STORY 6

Buried all around, lays intent never acted upon

STORY 7

A sun will rise on you one day and your life will become your escape. And in that moment, you may no longer wish for the other means that held you fast, for so long.

STORY 8

A cool mountain breeze, rolling in through the fog of a beautiful fall morning. Caressing the hills and leaves covered in all the beautiful tones of orange, red and brown.

A tin coffee cup moving from table to lips, as I fondly recall moments from just hours before. The book, in my lap for the now, opened and awaiting my return. The words begging for release from the pages, being freed to the world around.

Sounds of nature and silence, hovering all around. Dancing from reality to imagination and beyond. One however draws on my attention more than the others, a sound of knowing and familiarity. It pulls my gaze back to the now, so I glance up and further into the room.

And there she stands, the most beautiful love affair that never was, for it had never needed to be spoken of. Her brush grazing canvas, colours flowing behind. Forming a beauty of their own, not unlike her touch upon my soul. And I wonder, what masterpiece will she create upon me today……

STORY 9

When the words stop

Where will you be?

Could you watch?

As they slip away

Would you refrain?

For another day

Perhaps they come

In some twisted form

Not how they were

But mostly torn

From lips, most sweet

They fell to earth

Climbed to ears

To my worn heart

They surely meet

STORY 10

Time passed through
A memory of her
The scent in the air
Shampoo smell in her hair
I sank into it, sweet
Her smile I'd meet
At a crossroads, bare
My soul took great care
To cherish this treat
For her spirit I'd greet
When I finally got there
Again in our love
We would share

STORY 11

I began to wander

Aimlessly, around rooms

Inside a soul, reserved

With purpose and kindess

A slow pace, a measure

Of a man and his worth

STORY 12

In moments, pulled away

Thrown together

But never to stay

Or so it seemed

One fateful day

She took from him

Things, come what may

STORY 13

Natural never felt so unreal

She tasted like the rains

As they cleansed a soul

Of demons old

STORY 14

I thought myself right out of existence

And for a moment it seemed right

But then, I began to miss myself

Wished for myself, the bright light

That would lead me back

But too far gone, that night

Had I become

STORY 15

Our hearts spend time celebrating in all that is right. Our minds spend time searching for one thing that could be wrong. In the end, one will prevail. It is by our own hand, the outcome of the day.

STORY 16

Do not let me

Because run

So far, so fast

I shall

In the face

Of your grace

I shall

Bow to a will

By hand of own

And fear unknown

I shall

Wish you to hold

Me steady, in place

To stay a while

I shall

Not win the day

Versus the darkness

Alone, as it comes

I shall

Turn from you

And hide away

In denial of self

I shall

Struggle some

Dusks, some dawns

With presence near

I shall

Overcome

And rise

STORY 17

To rain on the happiness of others, one must first create a storm in their own lives.

STORY 18

Friend! Hold fast

But for a moment

Maybe two, or more

Let me hasten

To thy side

Will you sit?

May I tell you a tale?

Of my magic,

Weave you a spell?

For perhaps if you see

Where true beauty lay

Life changes course

Come, whatever may

It is the breeze

Through their hair

As you let them walk free

Their spirit steps softly

As they stroll

And they ponder

With thoughts, again theirs

Do you hear? The echo

Of them, as they speak

Listen close, one must

For they tell you of dark,

Of light and of trust

And although their form

Physical, is a sight

Of its own, to be bare

For you to share

Your soul they must roam

If your love be pure

Then show them

And again and once more

Make for them, inside you

A place they call home

STORY 19

You were the same dream

That I held, so many times

Dearly, in a space of pieces

Parts of me, undone

Fractured by a loss

That never truly happened

And yet it had, over

And again, borne by a hand

Of me, oh what luck

Look at the gifts he brings

A smattering of guilt

Portions of disdain

A shattering of days new

STORY 20

A storm in my eyes

Etched across skin

Of a weathered face

Is not the storm

That used to roil

The calm seas

Of my tranquility

Make no mistake

Its force is the same

Its will has changed

STORY 21

When the questions come, and they will, let me answer them as honestly as I can. Perhaps they will remain unsung but here lay your answer anyhow.

She is simply nothing to me and in the same momentous sip of time, she is exactly everything to me. She is the sun on my face, the rain in my soul, the wind across my tired skin that feels like the breath in my lungs. The breath in my words.

Her cosmic chaos surrounds every fibre of my being, bringing sparks from beyond that pump life into each pore they happen to dance upon. Lightly, across my presence, each one an assurance of life.

Never before had I been so open to anything so pure, untouched by the hand of man. You see, I shall not place a game of words to it. For in these moments, man has a penchant for fashioning prisons out of those words. To harbour and possess the most beautiful of things.

Free, she shall always remain. To ebb and flow as she wishes from my life. And upon each removal of herself from I, awaiting the next return patiently, is all that shall pass. For when her spirit is free, the gifts she offers of self are greater than those I could wish for.

My steps around this peaceful and calm place shall forever more be as measured and silent as possible so as to not disturb the innocence of it all. I have wondered from time to time, if she notices me there. As I do. And then I wonder no more.

For in these places and moments you see, it does not matter if she feels the things I feel. The only thing that matters is she allows me to exist here, in my contentment. She is free to draw on me at any time, for you see, she is always drawing on me. Painting at every turn, the most wondrous designs within me.

My loyalty to her shall never pass, not with time, and most certainly not, with any words another mortal has to say on the matter. I am bound to her by a thread, invisible but stronger than anything most people could ever imagine having graced their lives.

It is by choice that she brings her gifts to me and it is by choice that I run to her. And in that secret, lay everything you ever needed to know.

STORY 22

If this is my madness, I think I will lay a while and get to know her. She feels like bliss.

STORY 23

Stop living and start dying!

I know...I know. Bear with me a minute or two. For me, this is just one of the most recent shifts in perspective that has led me down a path to some very real fulfillment. A secret of my own.

It came when I had finally reached a peace and calm with my own mortality. We are all spending days trying to 'live our best lives' and hey, if that alone works for you, amazing! For me, I found that if I was always looking to the next day to be there, that I would procrastinate on many of the things I wanted to be doing. I could always do them the next day of living.

Now that I am spending my days dying however, I am doing all the things I wish to be doing. It has also led back to an appreciation of things as simple as a breeze through some leaves, the smell of summer in a forest, the sun reflecting off water.

My hope for each of you, is that you find your own versions of this, more quickly than those before you. Why wait till it's 'bucket list' time?

Start checking those boxes in your soul now!

STORY 24

Echoes of carelessness

Roam the dusty chambers

Of a heart stuck

Perpetually broken

Searching, begging

For a touch in kind

For the days remainders

STORY 25

You said you knew

I believed it true

Alas, it shall not be

For I shall not soar

On wings not free

STORY 26

She asked a simple truth

And yet, all I found

Was silence..followed

With, but a standard reply

For I had decided, me

And who was I?

That she was not ready

She would not understand

Feared too much, I did

That she would hide away

If the words I spoke

Rang true, but perhaps

Were spoken too new

What a coward am I

For she looked in that moment

Like the heavens I knew

She felt like a presence

That could pass through

Tasted on the tongue

Like so many words new

Warmed a soul, akin to a fire

Of nature, of life

Wearing nothing but blue

Smelling like freedom

STORY 27

Until the day

I took a step

Nay, two or more

Behind, removed

Startling simplicity

Earthern soul

Ablaze, drawing

Dancing light

I had never seen

The simple truths

She bore, she wore

For weary eyes

STORY 28

The smile she wore
When the music flowed
Through her veins
Was so full,
Youthful exuberance
And an abandon
That I wished for,
I came undone
I could have fallen
Into that grin
For a thousand lives
And never tire
Of doing it all again,

Thank you for being

Nothing and everything

A universe,

In motion, behind

A smile...so simple

STORY 29

Oh, how you look

You look, do you see?

Watch as she glides

Across the page

Of her earth

The colours that run

From the trail she leaves

Behind, mark the ground

As you scurry, after

All that you offer

Are whispers of poison

For a spirit so free

In hopes that you

May plant in your soil

Her roots, sure to spoil

These hearts beat for truth

She will always be seeking

To find the source

Of the sun and the song

Inside, burning so bright

Serenading so long

A chance once, you had

Yet a cage of man, offered

And now, nothing but to fall

To your knees, along side

The cracks of dream, desire

In asphalt they remain

To remind men, refrain

To prove man is no god

Prove to me, all I ever was

Hoped to be, to free

Was a fool

STORY 30

Did you not know?

My twisted heart

Would simply not rest

Could not beat its best

Until I captured it

Wrote the colours of you

Weaved your essence in to

The stained pages of me

Turned into the chapters

Of a life running free

STORY 31

After all the years past

Did my best to live again

Tried to find the path

That led to love again

Live and love with no fear

For all my wasted effort

All i was left with began

With no trust in you

For everything, anything

That i held most dear

STORY 32

I find myself cursed with a heart that whispers poetry, ever so softly. Yet, also blessed with a mind that will not allow me to follow those trails so warm and comforting. I simply cannot translate into being the things I feel inside for all the people I have claimed to care for. In all this comedic tragedy lies good intent and a man trying to humble himself before you. Forgive him if you can, his time may pass before a change so deep can be processed.

STORY 33

The way in which

I chose to wield

The words I knew

Against the world

Against my love

The love for you

Brought forth a look

That now grew

Upon a face

With tears new

STORY 34

You had been

A sanctum

Supposedly

And yet a

Sanitarium

Arose in you

I bled out

My thoughts

The constructs

Boundaries

And limitation

Gave way

Something new

Nothing worse

STORY 35

I sang for you

The music inside

A melody so dear

Heart and mind as one

A soul, crystal clear

And then I imagined

That you heard me

Felt the lines of me

Wishing you near

And became forlorn

With realized fear

That I sang in my head

Once more and the last

Not one shed tear

STORY 36

The days had grown grey
A shade darker than the hair
Upon my head, more silent
Than an icy glare
Had never missed you at all
And now, you are never there
I wonder and worry some
For just who the blame will wear
Like the crown, thrown on a ground
As I watch my fragile ego bare
The moments lost, so few new
Nothing honest enough, to bear

STORY 37

I could not find words

Nor action, for cowardice

Would surely step in

Take the place and reign

Over and over, tumbled

Through a mind tattered

Like a flag of honour

Thrown on a ground

Paved with the illness

Of my very own device

STORY 38

How did I ever allow?

…….you to feel…….

So small, for all of

…your worth…..

Your time……..

I could not find the line

….to walk…to love…

You, in all the ways

….I knew….you grew

..without me….beside you

STORY 39

My disinterest fosters boredom
Which in turn leads me here
To find you, to watch, learn
Every nuance, each level that deepens
Upon your soul, that which you show
Those vibrations you let loose

And when I make them my own
You will find your bearing inside
Believe it to be true, no clue
As to why or how I see you
So clearly, hold your soul so dearly
Yet when I grow weary and turn
Away from that precious heart
The only question now left
Is to how you never knew
My true name, my truer game

STORY 40

You are the balance to another soul, the guardian of their faith. They will not arrive dressed as you wished them to be but adorned in beautiful scars. It shall pass in the moments where you have found peace and contentment within. Until such time, you shall not see clearly, the compass of another.

STORY 41

I heard your truth but would not accept it as my own and now I find myself walking the cobbled streets of unknown, alone.

STORY 42

Tell me, dear friend

Did you hear disdain?

Feel inevitable end?

Sing that old song

That one you blend

So well, for so long

A victim, the trend

STORY 43

If you don't believe in magic and love, then you have never seen beyond my eyes while I dream of you.

STORY 44

You gaze and breathe, in the most magical way imaginable. Music and colour stream from the only parts of you that matter.

STORY 45

The lowest cost of you

Was more, than my mind

As simple as it was

Could solely bear

Your speech, never free

Had attached, it's own fare

I brought silent strangers

To watch, listen and hear

To remind me of when

You roamed, simply too far

That you never felt so near

STORY 46

You asked about empathy
I showed you what i knew
Of that strangled notion
You wished for understanding
I brought the knowledge of you
To a carefully dressed table
Where i looked as delicious
As the food that I presented
You never noticed it was as plastic
As the mask I had chosen to wear
That evening you shed the wall
In the name of that faceless desire

STORY 47

I could never find a way to make you understand or believe, so instead i will find the means to send you away.

STORY 48

Sometimes happy is being right but sometimes it is doing right. And finding the happiest me is in learning to tell when.

STORY 49

Our colours bled across a canvas
Of our own device, silken fabric
Caught and trapped the tears
Inside glorious patterns, weaved
By intent, with purpose fresh

STORY 50

Keep moving forward

Those are the words

You have heard

Spoken again, too often

And you move, one step

Turns into two and three

But the weight of others

Begins to creep

Up, on to shoulders

Not meant to bear alone

A soul too kind, left

Behind by choice

But i see you screaming

Silently, slowly drowning

In a dislike of your fear

To show the world

That even you need a hand

When your knees weaken

From all that they are

All that you wish for them

STORY 51

For if you are not you

Then who could you be?

And when the brick tumbles

From its perch, shall we see?

That you were never there

Not once, were you me

STORY 52

I did not know where to start; we had become so torn, so lost to one another. Yet, in those darkest of hours i knew you would return to my side. So, i waited, with a patience most cannot fathom.

They see only what they want, only what they desire. Sometimes it makes me wonder just how easily a seed planted takes root in a soil not fit for nurture. They lust after the words they do not understand. For they have no bearing, no sense of a past that brought me a future.

STORY 53

You did not notice

The smile that landed

Across lips that sang

Your name, hushed

In whisper...for you

You looked right past

And they felt defeat

Like purpose lost

But you did not see

Reflection of them

Standing in shadows

Cast by your grace

As you swept past

Beyond the reach

Of a love never turned

The rock that they are

Eroded by the fluid

Of you, as you seek

The other in those

Muddied waters

I believed to be real

STORY 54

Just go.....but stay a while
Walk with me here, lost
Found the sweet touch
Of you, in my own denial
I'll linger far too long
Never here, rarely there
Over yonder, in torn smile

STORY 55

It made me mad, the thought of it all
That i was not as strong of character
As you had always shown to be
It made me so angry inside, how dare you?
Be so much better than me, no
I would break you down, bring you down
Lower my boot to your neck
Try and drown you in my insecurity
For who were you? To be living that way
When i was down and out, scared

Searched for you in this low place

But did not find, come to me my dear

Let me touch you with my hate for myself

Touch you with my darkness and fear

STORY 56

A brief letter to myself:
Please remember that it took many years over for that new person in your life to reach these milestones.

Feeling so completely broken, alone or worthless

Being so torn between any decision because any decision meant swift and destructive reactions

Having their faith in humanity stripped from their soft souls slowly by agendas

Having a trust so shattered they could not be sure how they ever would again

Fighting demons every day they knew existed out in the world and even ones they never expected

As you step forward carry with you some light luggage.

You are not anyone's saviour. Some are not ready to begin saving themselves, some already are. Some require assistance in doing so, some none at all. Some require no saving at all, they are doing just fine on their own. Your appearance in their world does not magically make everything better, so show patience and understanding. Sometimes all they need is to know you will keep existing in their world. Some just require you to be the light in their dark. Do everything you can to learn to distinguish between these places in ones life.

Believing you are right and doing right are two different entities you will find residing inside. Loosely quoted lyrics from a band should warn of finding yourself 'on the right side of hell but the wrong side of heaven'

Do your best to learn to hear people, listening is too simple and easy. People will normally tell you what their spirit needs, if you pay close enough attention. Most times it comes without words attached. You cannot truly understand ones soul until such time as you open yourself to them

Learn compassion and kindness, the sources to be taught from are never ending. No matter the struggle, all people are worthy of you stepping lightly around their soul, mind and heart. Everyone is just living their reality and own truth as best they can. Sometimes they are victims, sometimes they just believe they are. Make no distinction here, for both are true to them.

Sometimes people will 'drain' you, let them. You have no idea why they feel the need to feed on your energy with such hunger. Sometimes it's not for you to understand. There are enough people in the world who will help recharge you. Do not confuse this with not having boundaries for yourself.

Do everything with no price tag attached, never with a cost to another involved. Or do not bother doing it at all. Sometimes inaction is the best course of action if you feel there must be some sort of reciprocation. Put yourself aside, your chalice will feel so much more full in the long run for it.

Lastly, if you feel love…then just love! No matter whether or not you feel like they will in kind. There is nothing wrong with an unrequited love. Love them anyway. Love them aloud, love them quietly, love them when they are near and love from afar. Never rob yourself of love. Begin with yourself, move on to those closest to you and the next thing you know, you may find yourself capable of loving a stranger….another human outside of your world.

STORY 57

The scariest leap i ever had to take was from the cliff of knowing my worth into the sea of believing my worth. And as i entered those waters, this beautiful universe washed over me and i realized for all your weight, you would never drown me here.

STORY 58

If you did not teach me

How could i know?

The things you needed

Things i sought to sow

You showed me your heart

But forgot to walk the path

That would lead me slow

Down through your garden

Through all the leaves

Blanketed by our loves snow

STORY 59

As the days grow long

And time moves on

The new thought dawns

That i have become

My very own sanctuary

In my fortress of solitude

This tree, shall no fruit bear

By forceful hand or will

But by simply being

Will i become open, true

STORY 60

I fear a day has risen where growth is no longer achievable without destruction. Not that romanticized and sweet destruction of oneself as you become a better person either; I speak of malicious intent, the kind that leaves a wake of sorrow and regret in your path. Neither of those borne upon my visage, they shall be owned entirely by you. One may argue that this is not the growth one should be seeking out and in that, they would be correct. Yet i did not search, this poison found me wallowing and lost. The wound was ready to receive the infection it brought. I eagerly accepted it as my own as it promised me the light of a new day, a finer way. Now it manifests itself tenfold and slips me further under the warm blanket of its darkness. I can no longer resist; as i give in, a smile escapes my lips. For now i will show them, i will show them all just what it means to love me.

STORY 61

I misjudged my own intent and released you back into the world, where you then became lost to me.

STORY 62

You asked me to stay
To never leave, you lied
I could have believed
But i saw with my own eyes
Your truth swallowing mine
Your pride; shown, too divine

STORY 63

I fear i still fail at the easiest thing in the world, loving you.

STORY 64

And in you, i found the happiest tears my eyes had ever known.

STORY 65

For the first time in a long while, i thought about giving more than my heart. I contemplated giving my time and it made me smile; a warm, fuzzy and foolish smile.

STORY 66

She flowed so effortlessly across the canvas of my mind. Each stroke a masterful blend of brilliant colours that brought the edges of peace and tranquility together. Her brush, gifted with grace and poise, created a space we shared for a moment or two. A gift filled with expression and honesty profound, i marveled at the wonder she found.

STORY 67

My eyes started to realize all the sweet lies you told my hungry heart, so i closed them to shut you out but you slipped through my lips with your kiss instead.

STORY 68

Believed you were real

So long, it became true

Turned out you were smoke

And mirrors, a trick

Of mind and desire born

Through fear i fashioned

Knit together with glue

Of love, had once bloomed

Where my lies now grew

STORY 69

When the day comes that you slow down enough to notice someone filled your chalice with respect and you have your first taste true, you will never again thirst for attention to do the same.

STORY 70

I dance with my new demon of the day, while the song of my best intentions plays softly in the background. We sway together, tightly knit like a sweater most comfortably bound by fabric of ego and pride. It stares lovingly at me as it slowly devours a fresh dream that had tasted so sublime to my palate not so long ago. "Not today" it whispers "But perhaps tomorrow you will be good enough, strong enough to walk away".

STORY 71

May the winds of growth and change forever be the breath in your sails.

STORY 72

If the dawn never breaks

Again for my broken soul

It will be okay, i saw you smile

When that sun does not rise

And touch my tired body

It's okay, i knew you for a while
For those of you who stayed
When i did not even try
With you, i will walk the last mile
Of my heart, the walls i plaster
Pictures and sounds of you
That pulled me from my denial

STORY 73

Oh, how the fire raged on
The most beautiful flames
Danced and weaved a tale
Of all that she was, is
Soon will be, in a presence
So freeing, so undemanding

STORY 74

My sweetest inability

Found me spectating,

What once was an us,

Completely alone

Wondering where you had gone

STORY 75

A shadow of me

Stood at a precipice

Of longing and need

Turned collar to breeze

Coughed dust of a day

Let it bring what it may

For love, i will flee

Time, wait and see

STORY 76

Her biggest mistake was believing he would help carry her dreams when they became too heavy for one. So she set them down when the weight buckled her knees and in the moment that she lightened the load she began to fade away.

STORY 77

........And in you, i find my truth, my reflection. The one i projected upon your soul, the one i mistook you for.

STORY 78

That special sort of kindness

That leaves me lost and hurting

Your particular blend of love

That leaves me found and reeling

The kiss, left me bound and kneeling

Before your sweetest intention

Wipes clean a slate, so muddied

Leaves me cold, warm and feeling

STORY 79

Those ill fated questions
That escaped lips parted
Left attempts half hearted
We lingered and lounged
Waiting for the other
Wishing for another
Day to dawn, clearer
Than the foggy mirror
After the shower ran on
Wet with broken dreams

STORY 80

Grass blanketed by leaves
Stretched out into sky
Blended of steel grey, blue
A smile flirted with
Skirted the edges of
A disaster born true
Of intention, most kind
Played dimension of mind
Where pretension once grew

STORY 81

Live and love the pages of your life present. Reminisce fondly on the chapters past, the epilogue will soon be written for us all.

STORY 82

Had you never been unkind?
With so much purpose
You stole my words, left me blind
Without so much a thought
No seeming presence of mind
Of all the beautiful things
That waited ahead for you
Oh, how you could have shined!
Instead the ashes of darkness
Were all you had mined

STORY 83

The blurred reflection of me
A perfect projection of me
Glimpsed back from your eyes
Whispered lies from your lips
That sated me so, elated me so
Took me back to a shadowed bank
On that river, the place i would grow
Into part of the person you know

I wonder now, if you truly knew
That you would be one of the few
Then what could it mean?
Would you love me unclean?

STORY 84

As i sit here and the snow falls
Shadows feverishly dance around
The places of light left inside
And i realize that i never was
And undoubtedly never will be
Any shade of a person true, to you
I would be failing, always falling
For i would never feel complete
Never full, in understanding us

STORY 85

She longed for the day
Where her heart and mind
Would mirror the fire inside
Before the flame flickered
And began to wane too soon

STORY 86

She sowed the many fields of life with a smile she found so awkward. Yet to the ones who saw like me, those smiles meant a harvest rich in certainty.

STORY 87

A fractured storm

Stirred behind eyes

Serene but sincere

Waiting for escape

Approached by heart

Once held most dear

STORY 88

A smile found her, led by a mild amusement and a curiosity. She let it linger longer than she remembered she could and it widened on its own.

STORY 89

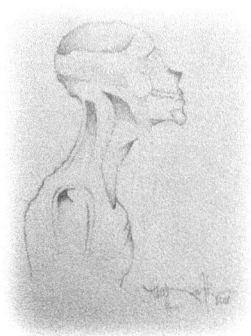

What use are my words?
If i do not lend them voice
I could of explained how i felt
What good are my eyes?
If i choose not to see
All the moments i left you weak
What good were the ears?
What purpose all the years?
If i chose to not hear you speak

STORY 90

Her lips parted and what came forth were not words but a beauty that nurtured the earth on which she stood.

STORY 91

Foggy memories loom

Threatening the day

The day you do not return

To me once more

Light and darkness war

In an uncertain future

That makes me question

What it was ever all for

STORY 92

Would it be okay if we were the only two who knew? Should it matter then? Could we shed the stigma of it all and feel happy, feel free in the moments to pass? To indulge in you, to explore the places left untouched for too long. To be whoever you needed during the darker times, waiting for them to pass. The thought has scurried by now and again, fleeting as it may have been, it begins to take its own shape. I wonder which monster it will become.

STORY 93

Hope for the brighter days, dims

As the wick that was us flickers

It wanes in the darkness that floods

The plains upon which we built

All of our foundation, led by belief

That it would stand the test of life

Laid before us now, laid to rest

STORY 94

I had never fallen into you believing there was an end....you said you had been waiting for it all along. And now, now we have arrived.

STORY 95

I unraveled myself, looking for the answers so long, that in turn i became lost to the person i once knew. Now i am unsure if i have grown or just led myself astray.

STORY 96

I had never felt so insignificant as i did in your presence. Yet, it was the most warming touch upon my soul in the very same moment.

STORY 97

She took a wrong turn and found herself in the most wondrous place of her life.

STORY 98

You wrote beautifully
The words of you
Upon my broken soul
And a most wondrous
Mending began inside
It reached all the way
To wounded eyes
And lips drawn tight
You etched your name
In my spirits old grain

STORY 99

She pierced his darkness with the light in her gaze, tore right through without hesitation. His resolve never stood a chance against her will, most beautiful in the simplicity of her love. Not a scar remained untouched as a wondrous warmth washed across him, cradled him in his own vulnerability.

STORY 100

Take me home, please
Back to the scent in the cool air
After the pleasant rainfall
Back to the smell of her hair
The breeze through the trees
It feels like i've never been there
The lakes of promise and need
I've wandered off the path, where?
Lead me back to eyes that bleed
The tears of love most clouded
Tinged with guilt, hurt and despair

STORY 101

She calls to me with the most beautiful melody. She is all things inside me, the winds and the rain that wash clean my soul. She does not arrive in black but shrouded in all the colours that make me weep for a time, a time that has passed, the moments new. I fear we have been calling her by the wrong name for far too long, spreading tales that are just not true.

STORY 102

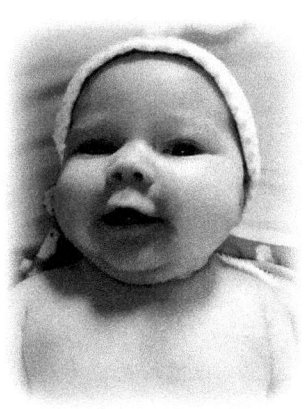

A breath was taken

Eyes widened

With a quiet wonder

As a cry rang out

Filled with confusion

And yet a sound

Familiar and near

Softened a shock

Cradled her dear

In a warm blanket

Of a soothing touch

STORY 103

She found herself standing
At the edge, always at the edge
Whether it be the boundary
To sorrow or happiness old, new
She found herself an observer
To the very life she called her own

STORY 104

Gazed off into the distance
As clarity set in, deeper
Than the pools in her eyes
And depths of her soul

STORY 105

The mystery that i am to you

Will never be solved by a refusal

To look beyond what you see

All that you cared so deeply for

Was never even remotely me

STORY 106

You could not have shone brighter while i clung to my darkness with a desperation so damp. Waiting me out with a patience unmatched by all who had stopped before. Their offers of kindness and empathy, pools which seemed to run dry rather quickly, as i did not adhere to some preconceived notion of timelines. In this, i found a love for you that ran so much deeper than any i could have previously believed in. Not the kind that poems, songs and paintings sang of in rhyme, with their romantic notions of time. A love that speaks to me on a level i did not think possible, a love that helped me home.

STORY 107

I could never find the million ways to thank you. There are just not enough words or acts to go around but when i close my eyes and think of it all, i smile. And in that smile i find you walking beside me, waiting to share your kind soul. The thoughts that flood my mind bring yet a deeper smile, that bores right through and warms my cold nights. This is the true gift of having you in my world, the wonder of it all could bring me to tears if i linger too long.

STORY 108

She cried the most beautiful tears

For the very first time, she found

A place to lay her head, where she felt

Finally, good enough for the world

Finally, good enough for herself

STORY 109

She took her time, sauntering ever closer in my mind. Crossing shadows that retreated under the warm light that emanated from within. Frozen in place, i waited with a sweet anticipation for the gift she brought forth.

STORY 110

You slipped away into the dusk of the universe we had created together. The last few strangled breaths barely managing to escape my grasp. I instantly mourned your loss, even though i knew you would return once more in a new form. Counting the minutes to your arrival would be a numbed pain i had known many times over. A small tear would form where it should, if only it could.

STORY 111

Excitement danced through your eyes
A universe hidden within, collides
Against the stars in night skies
Borne forth upon whispered replies

STORY 112

The sweetest misery my lips had never tasted lay waiting in your soul. Oh, how i longed for it. How i longed for you. How the thousands of miles seemed determined to keep it from me. Yet, they had not realized the strength in my resolve. For i will travel to the end of myself to know you once and kiss your spirit in more ways than one.

STORY 113

Skies darkened as clouds gathered
My tongue and hands bound
I lost you to the world ahead
Felt like you would never be found
A thought, instantly filled with dread
My soul sank lower than before
To the ends of this forsaken earth
Glimpses of you i will hound
For without you, my spirit bled

STORY 114

A shame, for all the things it could have been. Us together, were none of the things it should have been.

STORY 115

I wandered through the wonder that was you, marvelling at the sight of the puzzle pieces as they came together. Showing a larger picture than the moment that came before. You painted yourself with the most amazing brush i had ever been witness to. Each stroke heightened the intrigue i felt rising, pushing me forward without conscious thought.

Stumbling around with a newborns delight, i smiled with foolish abandon as my eyes darted about, unable to settle on any one thing too long. My words returned to me once more, alas i only glimpsed them for the briefest of time before the beauty stole them from my lips and fingertips.

My only wish upon my exit, that you released all of you upon the world. For none of you was ugly, none of you should have been hidden away. In essence, you had only stolen from yourself and others the opportunity to experience you bathed in all the glorious colours that you had always been.

STORY 116

I strained the grains of you through the fingers of time and watched as both slipped away from my grasp.

STORY 117

The thought of you alone suffices to keep the hope in my heart beating.

STORY 118

Gazing deep beyond eyes

Into the story that was told

Not by words but a mouth

Lined by a grief turned cold

STORY 119

The healing begins where fault and blame end.

STORY 120

The darkest parts of you still brought light upon my world.

STORY 121

And in that moment

When the inner calm

Surpassed the beauty

They showed the world

A peace passed over

A soul long tormented

And they smiled deep

The first honest and true

STORY 122

I did it all, except for all the things i should have done.

STORY 123

I sat and waited…for you to place that next log on my spirits fire. And you did not disappoint, you never have. And you did not know, you never would.

STORY 124

There is nothing more fantastic to witness than a woman whose soul has been set aflame and released back upon this world. And who am i but a humble yet foolish match if i do not fulfill my purpose?

STORY 125

You reached down deep

Touched a heart, asleep

I lay, far too many a day

Too many games to play

With hearts, led astray

And promises not to keep

STORY 126

You will forever more be the sweetest misery my heart has ever known.

STORY 127

She entered his life with an ease unmatched by any of those who came before and in that nature of elegance he found himself wanting more.

STORY 128

Whoever you are, wherever you may be.....you should know that my heart aches daily for you. So much that it breaks for you. I need to feel the kiss upon my lips that tells me i am home. I need to come home like never before.

STORY 129

If the truth be told, i never wanted you here. I never really wanted you near and yet you followed. In the shadows, you were always there. I know i am definitely not sure when you manifested in my world but you seeped in bit by bit. Dripped down the canvas of my happiness until it became so blurred i mistook you as such. A mask upon a mask blinded me to your existence until it was far too late. And oh, how you drug me down…how i allowed it to happen. Waves of self pity and uncertainty became an ocean to drown out the noise that was rhyme and reason.

Some days i feel so lost in my own mind, never being able to settle in on a specific direction to turn. Cannot decide on a bearing on which to focus my energy. I fear i will lose myself soon to indecision and an anxiety that should be unfounded and yet, here it is. I turn in my head and there you are. I turn away and you appear again. My inability to will you from my existence makes me more anxious than before. When i shut my eyes i can often find reprieve from you, if even for just a short enough time to allow for a breath.

I wish you did not exist in the realm in which i had created for you. Prepared for you. This place could swallow me whole, feast on my fears and dreams. It should have been my saviour, this temple i built but instead i found you to worship on. I stay awake, hoping that each new day will be the day you take your last breath and i can reclaim what was once mine.

STORY 130

She invited him in

Invited him in a little more

And then once more

Just a little further now

All started with a hello

The pictures sent

The words exchanged

To show interest, intent

Measured, yet mellow

She began to relax

Into something new

Questions raised

By experience she knew

Her heart would lead

If just for a time

How long would she stay?

STORY 131

Memories rained down
Struggled to protect myself
From the damp and cold
That they brought along
And yet hope burned bright
Within, where a healing began
The edge she brought with her
Renewed an old life lived
Made a heart beat young
Once more, into a new day
Once more, into loves fray

STORY 132

Carried you with me

Far too many years

All the useless worry

All the senseless fears

How i would lay blame

It was all your fault

I hung my head in shame

When the day finally came

And it settled in deep

The secret you tried to keep

That i was you

And you were me

STORY 133

Darkness looms with a tinge of anger, rising from the places untouched. He senses the shift inside as it attempts to rule. The smile almost slips away from under his control but he deftly swaps it out for a brilliant transition into conversation with the lady who sits before him. He asks her of all the things he simply could not care about, the things that will bring forth the emotions within. She will begin to feel like she has finally met a man who truly listens to and hears her. Someone who gets it. She will not notice his true self staring blindly beyond her as he takes all the appropriate cliff notes, they will come in handy later.

This ritual will go on most of the night; him faking his way through interest, her falling farther into his greatest of lies. If only these paper women had the slightest of clues, what a world they could save themselves from. The lingering stench he would leave behind on their souls would slowly seep into every pore. Perhaps he was wrong about some of them, maybe they had caught glimpses along the way. He supposed if that had been the case that maybe their egos had just gotten in the way and they had fallen victim to the ridiculous idea that they would be the ones who he would change for. Or maybe they had decided that his paper facade was enough of a reason to ignore the signs.

He disgusts himself most nights at the perceived lows he will go to and yet the people whom he surrounds himself purposefully with disgust him so much more. He is surprised he does not find himself violently ill at the mere thought of the steps necessary to reach the destination. Oh, that sweet moment; how he longs for it. It does not reveal itself as he swats the fresh flesh of their ass hard enough to bring the blood to boil in both of them, or as he will choke them to the edge of consciousness as he enters them. It will come as they fall just far enough into him that they begin to no longer wish for a day without him.

On that day, he will begin unveiling his truth and his world upon them. Systematically begin the destruction from the inside out. Everything they thought they knew, everything they held dear, would fall. He would descend upon them swiftly, darkness dripping like the tears from their eyes surely would. He tries to remember a time long ago, when he felt whole without having to leave a hole in another. The real demon lay in the hunger for he would not be sated long. A passing pity glides by, he scoffs as he is no longer sure if it flies for them or himself.

She catches it in the air and sighs. He looks intently at her through the fog in his mind, her face remarks on the uncertainty of whether or not it was directed at her. He brushes it off as a passing thought to the work day and something a coworker had said. She blooms back into herself and their conversation that he is still not listening to. Poor, poor soul. She is already lost to the night of her own heart and desires. This one will be far too easy but it will still bring the truest of smiles to his face as he watches his work take root.....

STORY 134

The tiny, twisted heart

Taunts me with glimpses

Of a dawning day, bright

But the voices of night

Keep happiness at bay

STORY 135

As the sun came into view, it dawned on me that it had always been you. I had spent so long standing in the shadow of my own love, i had not noticed the flight of the dove.

STORY 136

I dreamt a million dreams but none as sweet as the velvet touch of your kiss.

STORY 137

I wanted nothing more
Than your heart to sing
Your spirit to soar
Tried and failed and failed
Waited for you to walk
Through the open door
That i stayed and held
But to the martyrs cross
You preferred to be nailed
My soul will weep the tears
For all the forbidden years
Never remember the smiles
Never allowed the hand
To reach, beyond the miles

STORY 138

All i ever wanted

Was to close my eyes

Have you disappear

Washed clean from mind

Somehow anger lingers

Because now i fear

The day has come

As i shut out the world

And you do not appear

And i hate myself

For ever wishing it

For ever willing it

STORY 139

With an elegance unmatched she stood before him. Feeling more vulnerable than she ever had in her life. She had never met a man who seemed to see inside her so easily and the thought was almost paralyzing at times. He maneuvered himself around inside her soul delicately but purposefully. Her steps and words became measured around him and even though she was shy naturally, she was not entirely convinced that was the only reason. Something about him seemed safe, like the warmth of a fire on a cold winters day. Something about him made her tentative, a feeling like he could wield knowledge of her like power. Timidly she attempted to sidestep revealing too much in a short time. She needed time to believe, time to trust.....would he wait with her just a while?

STORY 140

I delighted in my own sorrow, my mind being the greatest oxymoron ever.

STORY 141

Her soul began to sing as she stepped out onto the new pathway. It had been lowered to a whisper for far too many a day.

STORY 142

Rain fell against the window leaving no sound behind. It felt as empty as she did inside; it tore against the very fabric of who she was, who she could have been. Her hand masked her face from view, masked the child from the terror she knew. The darkness he had brought upon her had ruled so eagerly, burdened her life so easily.

STORY 143

As the world laid out before me and offered its fruits i hesitated and tripped over my own hope.

STORY 144

If only i could have loved you like i did in my head, what a wonderful dream life would have been.

STORY 145

In the clutter of all the darkness, lay the one thing that would light the fire in her eyes once again, hope.

STORY 146

Standing on the other side of the door she had fashioned from mistrust, pain and confusion she waited. She waited for the one who would understand all she needed was time, time to watch and to feel. Feel a trust in a love once more, feel safe in a space that should have been her home in another, in herself. Oh how she yearned for someone to see her, as she once had been, see the life that lit her eyes before. Before the tears stained her eyes and heart once more.

STORY 147

I closed eyes upon a day
It was with too much ease
You simply slid away
I chose myself to please
Just another love to prey
Upon, filled with my disease

STORY 148

I searched corners dark and rooms bright but not walked for many years for the person i remembered. Was the memory of him a lie i told myself to ease a troubled mind? A costume i wore from time to time to placate a most tortured soul? Had i fallen so far for so long that the damage had seeped too deep into the cracks of the life i had wanted to be living? I felt lost, so lost that not even a compass of magnificent spirit seemed like it would lead me back. Love, an idea that just seemed so absurd now that it filled me with disgust. Misery and self pity my friendliest of companions, always there with a hand extended. The pillars of my world now, they attempted to bear the weight alone. A smell crept into the area, i recalled this scent. It was not new but i had definitely thought it gone. It was the essence of another, a brighter time. Hope. Why would you taunt me so? Why now? Why would you be so cruel? And of course i followed my nose, wishing silently for it to be keen once more.

STORY 149

Seconds slipped away
Into moments became
Moments slid by my face
Turned hours into shame
As they passed me by
On a highway, called life
Wasting hours on the fly
Straining eyes, beyond sky
Wishing for those instances
Returning you to my side

STORY 150

I slid the blade of self truth in and slowly twisted, sending the last shadow of doubt to its oblivion. Watched the blood of understanding spill out across the floor built from planks of acceptance and disinterest. The purity of the dark pooling liquid soiled with empathy leaving a stain of disgust in my mouth. Clotting colours streamed from eyes like tears should do as sounds began to diminish, echoing from days just past and a throat run dry of knowledge to share. Laying silently to observe the calm in the chaos i had created. The exercise in futility to soon be ended, from which i would rise once more.

I had always bent the others to my will, it came as easily as cutting through the cloth of my very existence when the results had been less than impressive. The face i wore was that of a man, whole, living a life fulfilled. Inside, i spent most of my days plotting, devising ways to rip it all apart on a whim. The tools of demise fashioned from expectation and ego. A force of resolve cloaked in misery and pain that would not be shed, especially when it looked this good on me. I counted the moments until this days work would come to fruition.

STORY 151

Train the mind and heart to be kinder to yourself, to slow down the best moments in life so you can linger there.

STORY 152

To had been the reason you slowed your pace would have been everything to me.

STORY 153

He pulled you in with understanding but the cloak of deception covered all he touched far longer than you could ever know.

STORY 154

I entered my own mind with a smattering of trepidation, lingering a touch too long. Stepping slowly into a corridor i do not recall seeing before. The door swung closed behind me, i heard it latch as it blocked out all remaining light. Blanketed in darkness, the thoughts that had been haunting my day rose up to meet me once more. This time, they had the advantage and would surely overcome reason with doubt. The feeling, although not new to me, this time had morphed. Panic set in like never before, i felt the sweat begin to bead on flushed skin. "Hello?" came the voice and my world weakened a bit more.

STORY 155

She seemed so lovely and yet he could see the outcome as clear as he saw his own delusional scribblings on the walls of his cell, his soul.

STORY 156

A weathered guardian stands tall, looks out across the expanse before him. His time draws near and the exhaled breath grows raw. They used to gather and wait for wisdom to be shared but yet the words he saw before him never came. Would they learn from his history alone? Or be doomed to become a fossil of a day? Be doomed by words they never say?

STORY 157

He drowned in her grace
As she grew into him
As she grew into her
Wished for a taste
Of her strength, found
Nurtured by fear of a year
Passed with such haste
Another moment to waste
Would be the hope, near
In his heart she be bound

STORY 158

May the winds of life

Bring songs of love

And happiness sublime

May your hearts dance

Nights and days away

Whisper words in rhyme

Water gardens in bloom

Make for another room

Rejoice passage of time

Watching sun and moon

Rise in skies, grey and blue

With intent born true

Mountains, together climb

STORY 159

If it had been you

Would love burn true?

Or would it simply be

A created mystery?

One of want and lust

To follow heart, must

Summon the desire

That lit a souls fire

Razed a will, to ground

Chased a dream, bound

In a stubborn mind found

The way to another day

The anchor, another bay

Tongue drown, cannot say

STORY 160

His brush dances on canvas

Emotions colours run true

Fingers guided by a sight

His mind has not yet seen

Effortless strokes, paint runs

On a path walked on a night

In fields he's not been

For a conduit, ever so right

In life's dreams they shine bright

The artists grass grows so green

STORY 161

As the sun sank low on the day
She strode forth, heels in clay
Winds washed a soul clean
Wiped the scarred wounds away
Possibilities in eyes, stream
Endless options, a lucid dream
Fresh spirit leading, never astray

STORY 162

In the fires of heart be cleansed
In a dance of colours be drowned
A face once torn, no more be worn
Set loose on a path, most profound
Melt away lost layers, be born
The life anew, to thyself be true
Or the demon be me, the demon be you

STORY 163

In her i found a strength to be weak and my walls slid away in an avalanche so cleansing i felt my heart sing.

STORY 164

Who will stand by your side?
When the darkness begins to weep
Shedding sorrow as light glides
Begins to creep, yields to tides
Of colour that reaches heights
Can you fathom the nights?
No longer needing the break
From a dream full of mistakes

STORY 165

One would think that they would remember the day of their demise. The day that changed everything but all that remains is a numb darkness that clouds a memory. I recall the why and the who, yet no smell or taste of my life comes washing over me. Gone is the sky from my misery, the colours outside. A perfume so long known, the look in your eyes. A melody that played through to my heart from the speakers in my truck that day. All the things i swore i would never forget, gone with time, lost to me now.

They are wrong you know, it does not heal but with blanket conceal. The wound that remains behind hidden in shadows but forming a future version of me that i had never wished for. Sometimes, just sometimes, the newer you is a little better off, different but wiser and ready for a new day, a new chance. However, there is also the time you waited too long and found yourself seemingly so far beyond repair that you did not care to even try and return from the pit you helped create.

STORY 166

You gave up your voice

For a love, never to return

In kindness, never found

STORY 167

I stared too long and surrendered myself to the promise and the universe i created within her eyes. The task now lay in meeting the needs of the beauty i found, to rise above and beyond my own foolish fears. To cleanse my spirit i must first let go of previous tears.

STORY 168

Shadows of when and who

Danced across the moon

Tears of what and why

Made damp, the memories

Like the knife that twists

Cutting deep, bleeding out

My love upon the floor

That rose up to meet

I shall greet, my demons

This day bound and leap

Across the scarred soul

Of two hearts broken, lost

Walls go up, emotions frost

Bring back the raging fire

Upon relations ragged pyre

STORY 169

Tools of my construction
Build the world that leads
Always steadily and surely
Down the path, light and dark
Towards my own destruction

STORY 170

My fires of desire are as easy to light as they are to snuff out. This has been the ghost that haunts me so, the reason my soul taunts me so.

STORY 171

If you had heard, closed eyes

So tight, block out blood night

Bring near, desire to fight

For a will to move beyond

Things held most dear

Things built of fright

Tears cried, becoming clear

The pool of thought, a pond

STORY 172

Hold me close but not too near

Could never make a decision

Many a day or many a year

STORY 173

The answer should have been no but my soul whispered yes again and again until it breathed no more.

STORY 174

Hide away from self, for the horror has become the truth in darkened rooms.

STORY 175

My heart bled out a most astounding array of colour upon the parchment of my soul. A misery profound, one i would never recover from and yet i could find no desire to. Allow my spirit to stay and decline.

STORY 176

I pulled back the veil of perception and peered out upon the world with the sole intent of not seeing at all but instead feeling my way through. To paint my vision with senses sublime.

STORY 177

Your whole being rained down, the torrential downpour washing over me in the sweetest sorrow imaginable.

STORY 178

I gazed inward and did not recognize my heart. A stranger to my very own perception. Where in the journey had i strayed so very far from the path i thought i had held clearly in mind?

STORY 179

You stopped moving long enough for my desire to catch up. It had not been intended to be you but somehow the paths crossed and in your most beautiful soul i found a new dawn.

STORY 180

Looked up and glance lands upon a soul that shines so bright it blinds my fear.

STORY 181

As the darkness turned to light
Tried harder to find the night
Comfort in mist, obscuring sight
Weak willed, turn to you might
I find the way back to the right
Feelings found, feeling unsound
Inside now to you be bound

STORY 182

Fleeting is my love, sent down
From above, my throne so high
Perched in blue sky, shed tears
Throughout years, unclear
The path now blurred, so absurd
The love you felt, never matched
The day you knelt, for then i cared
For then i shared, some of myself
Revealed in darkness you see
The happiest i am, when you are found
Battered soul on bended knee

STORY 183

I slipped slowly into the pools of her eyes, slowly allowing the passion to wash over me. It tumbled down my throat, for a moment i surely believed i would choke and drown on it.

STORY 184

I do believe one will find the answer when they truly understand the question.

STORY 185

It should not have happened, the perceived perfection i had of you. For that idealistic image i held so dear burst in and out of existence so quickly its fire burned a hole right through.

STORY 186

To find the dream i held most dear, i pushed her far instead of pulling her near. For what i thought i should need would be the means to make her bleed.

STORY 187

I woke and you were not there, we had become parted in the darkened fog of our self made despair. It was in that moment so lost that we never measured the cost upon our souls and hearts.

STORY 188

For who stood before me in the mirror, if not the creator and destroyer? The road to my own demise paved with desire and mistakes that had only led me astray once more. Was it the mind or the heart i should choose to ignore?

STORY 189

Her sweet thoughts pierced the dark of his calm, she found him hidden away in the depths of his solitude. Attempting to flee further from his own desire, she gave chase with a kiss that hobbled him so.

STORY 190

You'll forever be the ash that blackened my heart, i failed to clean it all away.

STORY 191

I recalled the way it all went down. Every instance that caused that reaction in my face you despised so much. I saw it so clear, in my memories so right and now so blurred. The look of disdain so brilliantly smeared on canvas so fresh. It brought us ever closer to that brink. You mirroring my actions and i returning in kind once more. We never stopped to look at the ground as our feet were pulled forward without hesitation, closer to the death of us. It was as we tumbled over, screaming in pain, that i realized i did not hate you at all but with every ounce of matter that i am, i loathed my inaction.

STORY 192

Now that i found you, lost before
The newest fear is the day
I beckon and you do not come
For what am i now? Lost without
Your sweet embrace, craved
Like none before, lost soul
The smiles brought to heart
If i shall forget, lost words fall
To the ground without a sound
Bring me back, lost memory
Shatter my world, if you leave
Forgive me my dear, lost sight
Missing you in life, cannot write
The things i need to breathe, tonight

STORY 193

I glimpsed into you

What i sought and found

Brought fear profound

I was not ready at all

To heed hearts call

I ran, so fast and far

Before any chance to fall

Could come my way

I would not stay

In my own love unbound

For my soul would crown

Your place, spirit inside

I found my space to hide

Away from you, so safe

My own heart, i will not bide

STORY 194

Wounded that it was not I
The one to make you smile
The one who wished so hard
To be holding you close
So tight, in the night
Wanted with all my life, while
Standing by, watching his touch
Oh god, desired your skin so much
Learning to live without
The kisses he got to share
Heat in your gaze i cannot bare
Passion burns so bright
Feelings, like it could be right
If only, if only you would turn
Away from him long enough
To see my love, strong enough

STORY 195

I'm not meant for you
You were never meant for me
We are just two souls starving
Choking on misery unfounded
It never seemed to fit just so
So many questions wrapped tight
The cocoon of evolving in sight
Thinking if it were this way
Instead of that, then maybe
Perhaps, then someone would care
Someone, with us their lives share
The answer was right there
Nothing had ever been wrong
In heated search stay strong
For that was exactly it
The previous just did not fit
Light suddenly lit, path clear
Walking with purpose we must quit

STORY 196

Dampened emotions
Spill forth, extinguish
Souls fire, snuffed out
Turned off the light
Lost my way, into you
I ran, struggled to find
The person i wanted
Back to my life, more
Than the thirst for love

STORY 197

She spent most her days
Approaching from fear
Tentative steps hold her back
From seeing what the rest find
Her truth burns bright
But seems to wound her soul
She measures and corrects
The paths that should have been
Find her losing her way
Her spirit hesitant, lingering
The mind pulling her astray
Feeling like she stumbles
When gliding felt deserved
Had she not done well enough?
Where had she gone wrong?
Simply, can she hold and be strong?

STORY 198

I glanced at the clock

It's time again, ruffled blankets

Like the feathers of my heart

Hit the floor once more

Rise from peaceful slumber

Perhaps i never wished to wake

The broken promises

To a glued together life

That i had been the architect

Struck me as mildly funny

Tiny choices or so i had thought

Such a large ripple left behind

In the pond of free will

Choices echoed, mocking

Like a bird set free

From an imaginary tree

STORY 199

I followed my inner dark

Hoping it would lead

To better days where i did not bleed

All i found instead was the mark

Upon my soul, left stain behind

My excuse for behaviour unkind

The wound which time did not heal

No longer capable nor want to feel

My actions, pay me no mind

A passage home so hard to find

STORY 200

The biggest regret was not finding a way to wake from the dream of becoming a better person.

STORY 201

Hidden away in darkest corners of desire is where your truth lays, awaiting revelation.

STORY 202

Believed i was ready
Until i felt the dusk approach
Panic set in where touch had not
Reached yet within
Anticipation became drive
To rise with the dawn new
Fighting through once more
Your love, reason to battle for
Must reach before time is gone
Lend hand to skin of silk
Taste passion upon lips before
It slips into night of no end
Rules of universe to bend
Never speak of no reason
Left behind from season, past
I breathe so as to know heart
Born of gold, new start
I shall feel before i part

STORY 203

The night taunts me with echoes of a past that could have been a future.

STORY 204

Having the proclivity of attempting to think yourself into an answer will only lead you deeper into the woods. Instead, close your eyes, breathe and arrive without the added toll on your spirit.

STORY 205

My charade, ruined by the sweetest demeanor. The behemoth called love destroys all in its path, runs rampant without care for my delicately laid plans.

STORY 206

The pain looked so fantastic that i decided to wear it as the coat for all seasons, all reasons. I even strode into the midst of love proudly bringing it to show the world.

STORY 207

I fell, for what seemed like decades. Into the endless dusk of your love i tumbled and the dawn smiled upon me.

STORY 208

"But can you?" I interjected. "Yes, i can" whispered the unknown.

STORY 209

Your heart is the hypnosis
That blinds my will to resist
Your touch is the sweet death
That binds me firmly in place
Your song is the softest call
That escapes sweet parted lip
Your exhale of tinged breath
That fills my souls vessel
Your eyes, those that carry music
That find dance in faint step

STORY 210

My happiness danced off into the mist of the unknown and i followed with a youthful abandon i had not realized still existed.

STORY 211

The demons caught up and oh, how they could have been angels but it is far too simple to wallow in the darkness.

STORY 212

Become your own hero, shed the adornment of the victim for the riches it brings are truly sparse expanses where you shall become lost to even thyself.

STORY 213

The tears shed would never be enough to fill the shallow depths of the pool called a soul but cry them anyhow.

STORY 214

I am glad you grew so lovely
Chances by my hand were slim
But look at who you are becoming
A most wondrous of lady, seen
So proud i stand by and gaze out
Upon your heart pure and broken
You fight through things still
My love, yours at will, if wished
Still never got any of it right
But watching you rise, shine bright
Warms my soul, soothes spirit cold
Daughter of mine, follow heart
Wishes and dreams, it will be fine

STORY 215

The sun smiles upon bared skin
Air wraps my body comfortably
Kind, the grass grows green
Tall, like the trees that shade
Beauty in my eyes, behold
Wondrous nature in action
Bringing forth season welcomed
Most, of all the four, hope
Renewed, like the rivers rush
As the melt begins, heart
Warms, like the days ahead
Flowers spring forth, from bed
Winters cold touch falls dead

STORY 216

You were never a friend of mine, truth. You sought to destroy me at every turn, so i turned the tale to an advantage. Made myself the victim, created a believer out of me. And yet, i had created the circumstances that were no ally of mine but this was unacceptable as i was entitled to a good life. As my lungs filled with air, my world should be filled with joy and forget despair. Pass on to me the life i desire, i shall sit a while and wait while my ego inflates.

STORY 217

I covered my eyes and saw it clear for the first time. I covered my ears and began to hear in ways i could not have imagined. I closed my mouth and tasted the most precious fruit. I pinched my nose and smelled the most beautiful scent i could have wished for. It came together in glorious harmony and exploded into my world before the gasp fell from bewildered lip.

STORY 218

When you begin to see with the assistance of the music of life, a world takes shape that you never laid eyes on before. Let the colours collide and ride upon the ripples they make.

STORY 219

Careful, for the mask i wear is one of a person who takes great care. You won't feel unease, until the knife slides in with ease. My tongue is colder than steel, with words carefully constructed i will bring you to heel. In the game of love i do not play, in shattered desire is where i shall leave you lay.

STORY 220

You stepped forward

The halls brightened

At your approach, smiled

Colours bloomed across

Greys, blacks and white

Fates happiness, rejoiced

Took the clouds from sky

Shook the tears from eye

In the end, i knew why

STORY 221

Strained through your filter

Of what love should be

Leaves me on bended knee

Begging for sweet release

From the pained symphony

Chained to the walls of desire

Thought you would lift higher

With ease, my heart refrained

Instead of freed emotions

Left to bleed, on floor hardened

Wood, like the soul polished

Frolic beside you on the beach

As the sun sets and leaves stain

Followed my heart, silenced brain

STORY 222

The currents may pull you under but the melody of that most ravaging river shall set you free if you will just listen.

STORY 223

Not all who wander are lost but be weary, they may have wandered too long alone to remember what it means to walk in harmony with another soul.

STORY 224

Do not dwell too long in the depths of sorrow for you may become lost to another tomorrow.

STORY 225

Rising from the rubble of your heart, you steady yourself and prepare to build the next house of love upon a firmer foundation.

STORY 226

You threw it all on the line but you had no idea just how much a coward my heart was back then and for that i am sorry.

STORY 227

I found you in my smile

My heart as it beats harder

Lungs as they expand

With new found desire

Be by your side, every mile

Of the life you bring

That straightens back

Brings the glint to eye

Known true for a while

STORY 228

As she glimpsed in the mirror, she caught a fragment of her universe. Laid bare in her starry eyes, her scarred eyes, was the will and strength she had always heard others tell her she had inside. She believed now and smiled with the elation and knowledge that she was no longer bound by her self imposed restrictions and hesitations.

STORY 229

Lust collides with will
To be seen, to be heard
A most momentary touch
A most beautiful remark
Unimaginable coupling
As we lose to the night
Ourselves, souls bright
Spirit refreshed, thirst
Quenched in another
Desire flares, larger
Than possibly dreamed
And fizzled like fireworks
When we named it love

STORY 230

Strangled truths cannot escape
Pursed lips, try in vain to part
Lacking courage to speak words
That will hold the light inside
Would reveal me to the world
Around, bring you closer than before
Though i want you there, next
For i will also want you further
Than you deserve to be, intimately

STORY 231

I did not hear your scream as your desire burned, by the time i took care to see, it had extinguished itself upon my ignorance.

STORY 232

Explain away the years

For my ears, for my tears

Explain to me the return

To the years before the burn

Explain to them the why

After they begin to cry

Explain for us the when

Of this moment and back then

Explain to my breaking heart

The reason you drove us apart

Explain to many broken souls

Just why it has to end

STORY 233

Lost and searching

Shall never be found

Silent mind like night

Without falling sound

Down abandoned halls

Stand firm, new might

Sanity flows like falls

Of water over edge

Endless drop, no end

Pleasure and desire bend

Your will, your monsters

Stand, brace and defend

STORY 234

She reached out and touched him, washing away any thought of the ripples from those before.

STORY 235

My shadow betrays me
Wanders off, following heart
So blinded by intention
Desire mixed with hope new
Forgotten past, new tomorrow
Some of me remains behind
The part that relies on self
Not trusting, not believing
In the calm waters wished
For years, the peace needed
Had never found but now
Shows itself at last, late

STORY 236

Have you ever truly felt the showers fall down upon you? The ones that cleanse your soul and wipe the slate clean. They come in forms many, the real, the perceived and the imaginary. In shapes you may not see but oh, when they come, they come with the thunder so close that it brings you to bended knee. In their wake, the rain still falls but now it pours from eyes most personal.

STORY 237

Why would you lift a spirit so high, just to set it down so low and walk away? Only the cruel provide the fuel to light those fires and the will to extinguish them in one.

STORY 238

I began the search many years ago now. It has been a long journey of many years and quite a few tears. Not unlike others, it began with seeking purpose. As if i was bound to stumble across some great reckoning that i would then share with the world. There would be much rejoicing for sure, as i would have no doubt come across life's great mystery. Finally unraveled for all to marvel at and the thanks would be plentiful. Painful

For each great "awakening" that i felt i experienced, the void i had thought would fill in, remained. Had i still been missing the point of it all? Was it all truly cyclical? Was seeking the purpose of life enough of a purpose? That one becomes self reflective enough that at least being aware of ones own humanity is the end? Would there truly come an elevation of ones own spirit beyond that which we already knew? Oh, how these questions plague my mind some days. Ungrateful.

Some days, just existing in this beautiful and crazy unimaginable world of ours is more than enough for me. The wonders it holds in nature please my soul greatly. Others i twist and turn and find no peace inside, like that last piece of the puzzle still eludes. I look for it high and low, frustration sets in and i lie awake and slumber will not find me before exhaustion does. Thankful.

The time shall come, when we shed the skin we were born into. What lays ahead next is still open to debate and discussion, as it always has been and the weird part is, i have found this place in my life where i am ready for whatever that looks like. Whether i move on or not, the answer awaits me there.

Shall i know it when it happens or will i just slip away without ever realizing that i now know the answer? Will i be able to return to speak of it? Would anyone listen anyway? Thoughtful.

STORY 239

Hiding behind our mask is far too easy in a society that is happy enough to accept it as the truth. We allow for the falsehood to grow daily not unlike a vine left unchecked. If you truly want to feel alive, pull the one you profess to love from behind theirs and have the courage to step out from behind your own.

STORY 240

Oh, look how your heart flows
Against the current so strong
How you float through leaves
But do not stir the air around
Brought my head from clouds high
Back down to touch the ground
Carried with quiet step and grace
My fears you taught me to face
Helped shape the man i am
Helped create the space i found
Inside, you cleared the rubble
Of what was left behind for you
The broken me, you helped make new

STORY 241

Never feast upon an unknown love and expect to find yourself feeling filled

STORY 242

The irony is that the horse you were beating was not dead, not at first.

STORY 243

They moved toward me and everything else slowed down exponentially except my heart. I could instantly make out the smell most horrid upon myself. Love. Ugh

STORY 244

Heart flutters like feathers on wind
You noticed when i was gone
Placed first before your own device
Wanted you to be as happy as I
Wished my heart to be as caring
As my back was strong from weight
Carried on too long, helped shed
By your love, found myself freed
Colours of you shall i now bleed

STORY 245

Your words that echo on and on and on shape my future,
more grim than before the time i loved.

STORY 246

Admired by many, in the head

Of none, yet adored and crowned

By a hand of own, i shall rule

This kingdom of mine, my pride

Shall bow, upon my presence

How you have been graced

Rejoice, for i have brought gifts

Of none except myself, shall suffice

It is all that you need, assuredly

My, how i have been kind

To allow your gaze to fall to me

Gratuitous you shall in kind be

For all my faults, overlooked you see

Focus only on those i find inside

Yourself, shall be pointed out

Reflected from I onto you

Shall they grow and be watered

Shame you shall find in words unkind

Work harder to please the ungrateful

Heart, only warms when adoration

Lathered in layers, no end in sight

My ego, this relationship, a blight

Upon poor soul so kind, wasted

Effort to appease grows naught

But gardens, valleys and rivers

That shiver, wilt and die when touch

Reaches out by my hand and words

You looked for the best but found me

Your blessed luck, none so much

STORY 247

Light poured through, strained
Separated by what i did not know
Like counting the grains of sand
As they fell from your fingers
Parted by the space and time
Between us, a chasm so large
A love struggles in darks embrace
Fights to the surface of water
So as not to become drowned
By the time we did not have
The time that we never had
To reach the moment most needed
By two hearts, wishing to beat as one
Desire to feel you near, the breath
Of a heart falling to nape of neck

STORY 248

Sorrows you felt, were drowned
In shattered dreams that crashed
To the floor, made from harsh wood
Of sanity and logic, collided tears
Stained the boards, colours pained
You drug me down, placed the kiss
Of your fate upon my lips parted

STORY 249

Dark hours approach, silent
As cold as steel untouched
By warmth of sun or heart
Should they be held at bay
Desires strength true but stoic
Walls rise, in place of old
Torn down, a newly found need
Chance and trust given free
Choice words, emotions bleed
Your art brings pain and fire
Wounds that run so deep
The memories last, of hurt past
Triggers the trap i find myself in
Forever sprung it shall remain
To remind me of you, of the pain

STORY 250

I pulled back the drapes that protected my heart and peered out the window of my soul, hoping you would notice me standing there. You just walked on by, oblivious, leaving me to wonder why i even care. It may be better to love and lose than never love at all but nothing feels quite as sharp as the knife of an unrequited love.

STORY 251

By the time i awoke, you were gone. Lost to the promises of should and could have been, just another love gone wrong.

STORY 252

We are all but flecks of dust tied together with a will to be seen for the sum of the whole instead of each grain.

STORY 253

The song to my heart

Is your breath in my chest

The gleam in my eyes, so tired

Being known by you best

I laid down and pulled near

You, the bringer of rest

For your calm my stirred soul

At home in most loved nest

My warmth on days chilled

In your presence blessed

Left found wanting more

In your love to be dressed

STORY 254

Tethered to your heart, i drifted off into the expanse of the unknown with confidence that you were my anchor.

STORY 255

I wish my heart had the strength my arms did when i was younger, perhaps i could have been stronger when it came to love. Now all i have to do is find the courage.

STORY 256

Occupied mind, why do you haunt me so?
I wish only for the slumber, sweet
Just the few precious moments
That i need to close such weary eyes
What is this prison i have wrought?
Words and experiences of my life
Have sunk their claws in so deep
Shame on you, more shame on me
For allowing this structure to rise
Inside, unnoticed for far too long
And now it governs me as it sees fit
Shall i be the architect of my own demise?
In the days to come of future bright
Mirror my reality back to me
Deny it as my own again, too easy
The creation of my own truth i seek
To find the peace inside once more
To find the way to put the beast to sleep

STORY 257

Eyes bled the rainbow colours
Of a love and life in dreams
Spat fire of an angered pride
Etched with recognition
And mistaken belief for years
They urge you to care
To want that most forbidden
Of a love and life, mirrored dreams
Pull you in, whispered words
That caress you so
Do you hear my soul, it speaks
True rhymes, no more than that
Of a love and life so weak
Bring you near, feel the heart beat
Against your chest, in your mind
Wished upon hope, none bleak
Needed you now, to tell you
Of a love and life so blind

STORY 258

Shattered mirrors cannot begin to compare to the pieces of me laying on the ground, staring up at you with bewilderment. The image of our love looking back, shocked in the answer most obvious.

STORY 259

I reached the point of no return and realized just how insignificant that was, as to move forward, one could not ever look back and long for those times anyhow.

STORY 260

Could it have been the wonder?
Of it all, the coloured dreams
So splendid in their certainty
Unlike life so real and random
To be swallowed up in happiness
Bringing smiles wider than rivers
Running wild to the sea of joy
Freed of the bonds of shades of grey
Multiplying the wings i soar upon
Flying higher than i believed
Was possible, happening because
The gifts you brought, received
Gratefully accepted, your easy love
Given freely, inhaled like the air
That fills my lungs with breath
To speak of your beauty, inside
My head reels around, heart thumps
Harder than it ever did before

STORY 261

Broken frames of dreams
That should have been
Surround a heart that withers
Knowing that it arrives
Knocks for us all without hate
Without love, come to take
I fear i shall not make the day
The day i wanted most
To gaze upon your soul
Look into the eyes so pure
Feel the touch on skin
Find peace within once more
Instead i find anxious hours
Wondering why you were so far

STORY 262

Desolate rooms occupy the floors
The heart that used to beat for you
Pumps naught but dust and ache
I dreamed and wanted forever
But all i found was your will to break
It should have been beautiful days
So right you were in many ways
So wrong, the doors you chose
We followed your path for years
And were left behind with bitter tears
If we had the time, to find us again
Would we walk beside willingly?
Should we talk again of dreams and fears?
Shall it change anything we did?
All i find now is the blood red smears
It should have been beautiful days
So right you were in many ways
So wrong, the doors you chose
We followed your path for years
And were left behind with bitter tears

Started off with intent so pure
As all things love, we wanted it all
We almost reached our goal true
Got lost in ourselves along the way
The perfect picture, coloured and drew
It should have been beautiful days
So right you were in many ways
So wrong, the doors you chose
We followed your path for years
And were left behind with bitter tears
So wrong the doors i too chose
For we were good without those
And would have been left without
The bittersweet tears that shout

STORY 263

Colour dribbled down the canvas
The art that was you grabbed hold
Embraced the beautiful sound
That your spirit sung, your voice
Shaking in its delight more pure
Than the waterfall of your heart
Fed by the spring of eternal hope
Alive, burned the flame inside
Dancing across the stars and moons
Your desire pushes my will aside

STORY 264

You spoke the words, i found a hole inside myself, climbed inside and have never returned since.

STORY 265

To be the shoulder you leaned on
Until you learned to walk again
On your own, to love you true
From across a room, quietly
Your tears choke my breath
To lift you from the ground
The broken angel that you are
To guide your arm to your door
Your skin, so soft that it weeps
With the hushed fears of years
My desire, not your lovely kiss
Your body to touch, never my wish
To watch you bloom, in fields
Untouched by the pain of winters
Snow, melted by the warm hearth
Of your soul, your kind heart
Mended by the knowing, you mattered

STORY 266

I smiled, she smiled. We both passed by and went on with our lives. Sometimes the most unique attraction is the untouched and unspoken.

STORY 267

Did you notice the tears?

Did you care for my fears?

Did you really care at all?

Did you want to watch my fall?

Did you harken to my call?

Did you know that i loved?

Did you know that i shared?

Did you not find trust within?

Did you never even begin?

Did you see what you left behind?

Did you take time to remind?

Did you ruin it for those to come?

Did you really feel the pain claimed?

Did you matter as i thought?

Did you see the hurt in my eyes?

Did you know i still despise?

Did you do it all over again?

Did you feel your wrong?

Did you think it was fine?

Did you?

STORY 268

Embraced by shadow

Nurtured in darkness, sweet

Sorrow comes for those

Unaware, of the signs clear

Robbing them of the hope

They nestled to bosom, dear

The gifts received, not expected

What they wanted, lost to seas

Currents that pull and direct

Your vessels made weak

Built with misdirected hands

And will shaken by the night

STORY 269

To accept ones faults first you must realize that perhaps they are not faults at all but an illusion designed to keep you from loving freely. Fashioned just so from the fear of success, its master, your own mind.

STORY 270

Your worth shall not be defined by the blemish on your skin, the scar in your heart or the worry in your mind. Look instead to the light that illuminates the path that brought you forth. For that light burns truer than any words that ever took flight and landed upon your waiting ear.

STORY 271

A soft snow fall blankets the streets in solitude and silence creeps into the night robbing the voices of the right to be heard. He leans a seat back and exhales a breath which could very well be one of the last. The smile lands across his face, most welcomed in its return. It should be a night like this, a desire fulfilled. The beast inside that was not right struggled to bring darkness that the light inside would not allow. The calm waves of joy lapped at the shore that should have been littered with petrified thoughts but were barren indeed.

STORY 272

Written in word on crumpled page
To be the book never to be read
To find my worth, the beaten path
Roamed blindly along darkened hall
Screams filled with silent retort
Thread that binds you and I
Holds hope strong, new and brave
Driven forth by a passenger
On a dimly lit road of mistakes
Lost to the current of life, frigid
The waters be dark yet shallow
Not unlike the passing of hours
Minutes captured in frozen portrait
Paint drips across canvas of mind

STORY 273

Struggled to capture you when i realized there were no words capable of boxing you in and who was i to cage such magnificence anyhow?

STORY 274

She climbed out of her skin and into the light of the new day, blinding as it may have been. Feeling prepared to face down all the demons that rushed forward to drag her back into the pit she had allowed circumstance to create. No longer confined by the fears she had placed upon herself, her heart and mind began to sow the seeds that would sprout and tie together the broken shards of a soul once so light.

STORY 275

Happiness falls like angels

From grace above, so high

It rains down, in your faith

In your place, they stumble

Wings restrained by acts

Most humbled, in your face

I find the reason to believe

Your skin, the tears i taste

A smile in your heart blooms

Like flowers in a spring bed

The layers, begun to shed

In our love, he grows new

Inside a room of care

She bled joy out on to earth

Cried a million deaths

As he flew far from our hope

Left behind the scars deep

Stolen before the first light

Leaving you lost in the night, dark

Never to return from misery

Sleep now young heart, sleep

STORY 276

Dragged down to your side, i weaken

Left too soon, wandering blindly

Answers left veiled in clouded eyes

Swerved from a road marked clear

On a turmoltuous night be feared

A candle dwindles down, flickers out

Sobs afflict a body in kneeled prayer

Softly asking to be led home, whisper

On hushed winds carried forth, hope

Light breaks the dim passage anew

STORY 277

I told my heart to be calm but the thunder rolled through with an unstoppable force, threatening to tear it all down. My walls, held so dearly together with reticence profound. My precious guard, will it withstand the onslaught? To rail against the light, to battle my will for naught. The questions that bring plague to mind also hold the key to clarity if one should find the path cleared of the debris that confounds.

STORY 278

My dreams roam the blanketed plains
Mind absorbs my truest wishes
Whence the power they hold in heart?
Warmth seeps into colds refuge
To hold you dear, to feel you near
Brings the smile that lights the pyre
Upon which corpse, denies desire
You breathe a life, no knowledge had
Prior, wings of spirit lifted to heavens
Above and from beyond your gaze
I ran cloaked in shadow of love
Your truth brings light i shall adore
The lust that burns, forever more

STORY 279

You were the mists of the falls
Tied to the breeze unfettered
Time shall dissipate the want
The wanton desire dismissed
Obscured from my dreams
Bitten deep in the night
Freed by a love, torn into light
Do you hear my song sung?
Hushed whispers, lips part

STORY 280

Gliding thoughts, tucking wings
Diving down like waterfall tears
Fears lost to the night like love
Blooming in the sun so bright
A flower so delicate, so strong
Dawning colours bringing light
Smiles that dance like the sound
Of hearts finding their way
United, spirits entwined take flight
Borne on a morrow, wished to see

STORY 281

She appeared from the mists of his own device, opened her mouth and the words that flowed forth shook the very foundation of all he knew. He contemplated fleeing but her gaze robbed his legs of the strength they would require. Her energy eroded his stubbornness as surely as waters against the strongest formation.

STORY 282

You expected more, i expected different and in the end we lost it all to expectations.

STORY 283

Your touch silences twisting thoughts, calms the demons i do not show. How you reach beyond and bend light around the darkest corners, effortless. My soul sighs at the sight of your approach, happiness blooms like an early spring.

STORY 284

Cheeks turning to rose coloured ash, she turns her gaze from his. The smile upon her eyes relinquishing her secrets to the night. Beautiful shyness balanced by love, the longing inside to feel his lips against her skin a measured contrast to the urge inside to flee within. He saw all of her and she hated and loved it all at once, never before being seen for the art that she was. She glances up from behind hair tousled just so, hanging across her brow and bites a bottom lip as a crooked smile lands across her face and she begins to unlearn everything love had taught her until now.

STORY 285

Never feeling like you got anything right but you gave it everything you had and in that alone the perfect beauty of it all should have been found.

STORY 286

He rose from the ground littered with the corpses of all expectation and moved forward with purpose instead.

STORY 287

Did you not know? I wanted your love and admiration but i wanted it under my terms.

STORY 288

As the ego is shed the road to satisfaction begins to light its own way.

STORY 289

She reached out and grabbed ahold of anything she could latch on to. Yet, this time it was herself and her spirit smiled.

STORY 290

Fall:

A leaf falls from its perch so glorious, the skies begin to redden and brown. It casts its disapproving glance your way as it makes its way down. It would seem so late of season to plant and harvest, yet a seed of doubt knows of time no bounds. What lay ahead is a time for you of question and of a chill settling in the ground.

STORY 291

Winter:

Cast aside like the most beautiful wrapping paper after the gift has presented itself. Tossed away into an absence of emotion is where your fall takes place, leaving you breathless in its entirety. The colours begin to fade in everything you face leaving you dreaming of days just past, memories grow dark as you cling to the precipice. What has come to pass and what will come to bear mesh together in the twisted steel of the wreckage of everything you had thought was life. Cold days ahead indeed.

STORY 292

Spring:

Hope takes root once more, something inside begins to push through the soil of your soul. A smallest of hints as to the joy that lay ahead begins to bloom before your colourless eyes. Once more the music most natural begins to land upon your ears, wings are spread and it shall take flight in days new. A picture most beautiful begins to paint itself before you. A promise lays itself before your feet. Days of growth ahead.

STORY 293

Summer:

A season finds you in full swing, lounging in the admiration all around. The warmth of kindness and love touches your skin and your spirit just so, the glow it leaves behind tearfully beautiful in its perfection. It could not have come at a better measure of time, the life it breathes with its colours into lungs so desperate for air. Finding your smile in the simplest of things, in all things. Bright and shiny days run amok inside and out.

STORY 294

The next man who challenged her soul instead of complimenting her looks had better want to love what he would awaken.

STORY 295

Standing at a fork in the road
She finds confusion, a fog settling in
Her path obscured by the greys
The agony that experience brings
Either decision used to be drowning
In colours that weaved their way
Meshed so easily with her soul
To be thrown back in time to undo
A wish that lingered so
To find the girl that used to be hers
Before the man who simply could not
Not love like she had thought it would be
Nor see her for who she truly was
She yearns to feel the fire inside
The warmth like sun kissed skin
From days past, a bike laying askew
On the road to nowhere, life so new
Once upon a different time
Where her spirit would ebb and flow
Not unlike the tide in her heart

That now guides the feet and mind

Found a little unsteady some days

She pushes forth toward her goal

That which she offers profound

The solace it brings still so sweet

For she shall find that counterpoint

In another once more, brings hope

Her intention pure, her smile true

And the kiss to be found, the last

STORY 296

He should have fit in somewhere but he never truly felt like he did. How was it even possible that among a million souls barely a one felt like a match? The things that illicit emotion within him, he would be scorned for and scoffed at by most. Tears filled his eyes most days when he would find himself stumbling across the simplest of pleasures. Doomed never to fall, they hung in his eyes restrained by will and a longing not to feel weakness. The silence muffling the screams that would echo through the hallways of his mind. These dark and dusty corridors forbidden to all. He would associate himself with lost souls, the oldest of old who he found himself walking alongside.

Imprisoned within, wanting the warm shroud of acceptance. How would this come to him when he has not yet learned to accept fully the mantle of his own doing? He closed his eyes some days and would begin to drift among all the most glorious colours of life he could imagine. They would beckon to him, the sirens call too strong to ignore and he would approach timidly. Reaching out to touch the blooming foliage before him, trying desperately to shed the hesitation inside. Just as he begins to believe it is for him to fathom, they shrink away from his fingertips, turning grey and lifeless before him. This most cruel mockery repeats itself again and again.

He feels there will come a time when he loses the will entirely to reach out, no matter how strong the pull. Wondering if we are all just lost to ourselves and wandering aimlessly, seeking out a most blessed purpose that may not exist at all unless we will it into creation. The things we desire to most, just fictional movies stuck on an endless loop in our hearts and heads. The people we encounter, the screens on which we project them. If that were so, then we just need to choose to find the reel of film within, with the fondest of memories and hit repeat all. Left in our ignorant but utopian bliss for the rest of days. That thought brings a smile steeped with a hint of sarcasm across his face. His eyes light up with wonder for the most brief of moments. Oh, how his never ending maze of thoughts warms him so.

He leaps between the branches of his beliefs so effortlessly, new bark spawning daily and breaking free of the old. How is it so easy to feel so committed to something and then shed said conviction when the time suits ones needs? Is this an illness or a simple truth of human nature as a whole? Could he possibly stand alone in this or perhaps with a majority or minority? Supposing it could be what is termed as growth, he writes it off as such because it seems like it would be more acceptable this way. Has he discovered free will or a poisonous mire from which there will be no escape? Dancing across the plains lined with good intent shall bring him recompense for his soul he imagines. Or at least he prays it so.

Finding ones way while laying battle against oneself is a difficult task he finds, most likely a fools errand. Yet, there is something about it all, that also lights the darker corners of a spirit and somehow a trail emerges from it when least expected. He strolls onto it and is immediately drawn to the sights of his own machinations, unexpected to say the least. He laughs at the irony of it all, trapped by his own doings and yet a victory so sweet in its defeat. Would the faceless crowds cheer for him now or taunt him some more? Not that any of it really bears weight during the dusk of the day. He slips into some music of the most purposeful choosing, the sort that will allow the colours to return in an explosion so bright. The smile remains as he closes his eyes once more and allows his most beautiful mind to run off unattended into the night.

The most welcomed of feelings creeps across him once more, that beautiful warmth known simply as serenity.

STORY 297

Raise above the ever rising waters of life

Never dance like there is an audience

Dance like no-one else matters

Shake off the pains that grow with you

For they are only worth the experience they brought

Not worth carrying around for time eternal

You are beautiful and talented

You are worth all the good that is offered up

Larger than the terrible that drags you down

Beyond the reach, you will be free

Into the breach, you will stride unhindered

You can do it all, whatever you wish

Just decide and make it ever so real

They cannot hold you back with words of naught

There will always be the ones to hold you back

For they have not found their strength

Have not found their own wings to fly

It all lies within, the secrets of this world

The smile across your face, bring it forth

Washed away, shall it be nevermore

Your time is not tomorrow, it is now

Begin the journey towards the one

The only one who will carry you on

Bear the weight, effortlessly you shall

Lighten the load with a peace within

The heart of gold inside shall light the way

STORY 298

To reach out and touch you
To open orbs of green and see
To hear the whisper of your embrace
To me, what is meant to be
To find warmth against your skin
To be found dreaming out loud
To allow you nearer than the last
To drift higher than painted cloud
To find in you new hope
To find in me new season
To allow myself to believe anew
To smile foolishly, you the reason
To fan the flames so bright
To wander far but near to lust
To never lose but to find myself
To be closer to you i must
To absorb that which you exude
To be better because you inspire
To new heights of passion we bound
To walk beside you now, my desire

STORY 299

You thought you meant nothing

You were wrong

You thought you deserved it

You could not have been further from the truth

You thought they were everything

You did not know they wanted it all

You thought you did not deserve happiness

You fell into your own mind

You thought it would not happen again

You blinded yourself to it

You thought if you could just love them better

You gave until you were consumed

You thought you had brought it on yourself

You accepted this false truth as evidence

You thought that it was normal

You mistook normal for all too often

You thought to blame yourself

You punished yourself for failure

You thought you would matter more

You began to believe you did not

You thought you were supposed to fight for it

You drained yourself entirely of will

You thought you had to stick it out

You knocked yourself down again and again

You thought they would love you back

You were better off without

You were wrong to hate yourself

You were wrong to think less of you

You were wrong to believe in lies

You were wrong to shed those tears

You were wrong to try so long

You are wrong to care

You are wrong to worry

You are beautiful

You are worthy

You are everything

You are you

STORY 300

Left on the floor, broken
I saw the light of the sky
While laying on my back
That was your mistake
Your undoing, if you must know
To leave me hope in the night
The dawn showed you clear
Wiping away years of fear
Washing away years of tears
The horizon draws near
On it i find myself, waiting
Calmly watching, looking back
Upon myself with sorrow
For in your love, i lost my morrow
The day rises new however
And in my future found
You will be never
Never freed of the binds
You placed up on my heart
From here on in, i find apart

From you i need nothing now

My soul unbound and bright

You chose to lose

Your choice to fight

Goodbye to love, so long

I will look for you some time

When the time is right

STORY 301

Will you stand when it is all torn away, will you survive the darkness? Will you fight for what you want or will you abandon your desire completely? Will you rise above the sea of malcontent and find your way home or give in to the murky waters and drown in your sorrow? Will you know which choice to make or suffer in silence for far too long?

STORY 302

He breathed all her glory in, exhaled and melted away into the sweetest nothingness he could have ever imagined.

STORY 303

She was his tide, he was her moon. Pulling at her relentlessly all she could do was give in to the ebb and flow of her spirit and offer herself up to his night. In doing so she found she did not drown but rose above the waves of his soul and together they painted a skyline like no other.

STORY 304

He towered so proud in his love. He loved her like no other, for no other could love like he would. Wrong, it was all so terribly wrong. In her eyes he saw himself and he was all that he loved. Ashamed, is what he should have been.

STORY 305

Inhaling deeply, he took all of her in
Oh, how she tasted upon his soul
The sweetest sound, her music to his lips
Her eyes alive with the sun within
Drowning in all that she was
He had never dreamt this slowly
Each moment, frozen in passion
She saw right through, he shakes
Softly in her embrace
With eyes born new he waits
How quickly she takes it away
Fears wiped away in a gaze brushed with love
Thoughts lost to time, breath stolen
By a beauty so deep, desire begins its creep
The answer buried in the kiss
Truths unearthed by her spirit
She is the breeze in his skies above
The weakness in his knees
The smile in eyes that were once bleak
He had waited for this, waited so long

For the story to be told, for it to unfold
For what is a story if there be none?
None to listen and none to read
She would tell it again and again
Each day brought new, the sun rises
Upon him once more, lungs filled with will
He must stand tall and guard her heart
The heart that loves him well,
The heart that casts its spell
He can do no less for it is him so blessed
Her grace shines upon him
As he smiles and opens his eyes

STORY 306

You were the sound of my heart, coloured in
Bringing forth the best in me, in all
The hitch in my step, the voice in my eyes
It has not found me yet, the dark without
My heart still warmed, my soul warned
How could you leave me behind?
I believed in our love and why?
On that cold and dark eve, i could not cry
My words stolen with just a glance

In my tears i saw two worlds collide

The slippery road left us no chance

Know now in my bloodied embrace

You made just too much sense for it to last

One day i shall stand once more, for now

I cannot pick myself from floor, in stained eyes

You will remain forever, with love grown

In fields of sorrow i shall find joy

In your eyes so young the new hope springs

May she invoke your spirit in all she becomes

Will love find her soul planted in the soil of you?

May she learn never to break in love

May she know your heart and never brake in life.

STORY 307

He slips behind her gaze and into the expanse beyond, her universe so beautifully coloured unfolding before him. Instantly the wasteland hidden within his own eyes begins to absorb the treasures she offers so freely. The voices strained for so many years in memories refrained begin to take shape once more. He gently weeps invisible tears as he begins to unburden himself of the sorrow he had no right to carry for so long. It was never his after all, yet somehow he had let the cursed symbiote of guilt find its way to him. Every interaction had left its mark, his soul a scarred and lonely domain, once beautiful.

To create in another, the place he shall hang his head for a while, as the misery of his lonely crusade comes to a close for a time is a true gift. The only gift he had been given it seemed most days. Finding the vessel so willing to share of themselves was becoming increasingly harder with time. His soul craves slumber and love, yet he is spurred on with what should seem like glorious purpose. Endlessly moving throughout the mists of time, the mantle he chose for himself pulling him apart from within. The decisions he has draped across his shoulders to bear mock him without sound. He prays she sees it all and will love him because of it.

She stands before him, crossing leagues which know no bounds. She chose to chase down her happiness, not watch it disappear over a horizon unknown. Letting her heart win out for the very first time over her brain. Her core shaking gently as she allows him into her soul, where none had gone before. Her love had been growing wildly for a while now, running amok within but this is the moment that counts. This is the first time someone will touch her so deep. It was the only true decision she had left, it was this or allow herself to begin digging her proverbial grave. She had almost given up entirely on the notion of love until he happened into her life.

Fear of the unknown attempting to eat away at her emotion, trying to become rational and stop her in her desire to find her destiny. Oh, how the lingering feeling of a misstep now follows her. In this state, she is sure she will die a thousand deaths if he turns her aside. He calms some of it within her, some of it she channels back into excitement at the prospects of a future she has seen for herself. Leaving everything behind her on the floor, she has come to him. Vulnerable and stripped bare of her security she finds herself feeling the most brave she has ever felt in her life. This brings a smile to her heart, knowing at least that his intent is not born of ill.

STORY 308

Daughter:

You opened your eyes, the world so blinding at first. What you heard was lost to you then and i never said it right again. Not when it mattered most. I fell apart on that front, tried so hard to climb and mostly failed. That hill seemed insurmountable and yet it should have been a leisurely stroll to find your love. So many mistakes that i made, each one darkening the light within your eyes. I could see it going out and lost myself deeper to the resignation that i could not save it. This makes it even harder for me, knowing that with each misstep it gets worse. It makes the easy impossible for me, i choke on every attempt that would actually work and find only the desire to try less.

This is the worst gift i have given myself and you, when all you gave me was the best gift of all. Unconditional love and a smile that could lift heavens and shatter stars. I hang my head in shame, silently because even admitting it i fear most days. But now, now i face my remorse alone in the night and i hope my weightless words can find a new home in your heart. I just want to love you how you deserve, how it should have been all along. I want you to truly feel it, like you did before i ruined it for the both of us. I am not entirely sure i will ever even truly forgive myself and in that i find concern. If i cannot, how will you ever?

You ran to the door, your heart so bright and i closed it each time as i walked through. Each moment, i felt it true and i had no clue what to do with it. My last wish on this earth is not for myself but for you. I hope you find something in this life to bring that light back into your eyes. I remember it so easily, like it was a second ago. Your spirit shining through in everything you did. Every moment that i actually got to take part in properly, locked into my soul. Every word making me smile inside because you were me and i was you. I hope i did not poison that well too long, that it can be undone.

You are so young still and hope remains alive, that these words will fill your cup and help you find a better path to the knowledge that you are everything to me, even though i never be able to seem to express it like i can in writing. You are my child and the child i want to leave behind should be complete in love. You are worth each and every good thing that happened and will happen in life, you are not the bad experiences. They come to you without your asking, you did not deserve them. There is good in them though, if you look closely enough with eyes willing to see.

Shine brighter than you ever have before, in all that you are. If i can impart any wisdom upon you, follow your heart. Your heart and mind will rarely coincide and sometimes it feels like you can never stop thinking. In following your mind and the "logical" choice or what someone else tells you is right, you will always be left wondering what would have happened if you had gone the other way. They say following your heart always leads to happiness. Well, it may lead to wrong decisions and heartache too. The secret in the saying is that simply by following your heart, you will be happy because you did what you wanted to in that moment and your mind lay quiet. This is where the happiness can be found, that you made a decision and followed it through. It is not always in the end result.

I love you with everything that i am, broken parts of me and all. Be now who you should have been, can still be. The person you were meant to be and i will always be proud to call you daughter. You have never let me down, no matter what my words or actions may have made you think. You are my flower and hopefully this water does not find you too late. Shine throughout the night in the world, be the dawn to the dusk. Be fearless and full of ambition to go after what you want, what you love. Do not hesitate in what others may think, live your fullest life for you. Love huge and love long and true. My dusk will not denote your loss or failure but a new day about to arrive.

STORY 309

Wave after wave crash against the shores in his eyes, the will behind them beckoning to her. She had bumped into the cool steel of the table leg on her way out of the coffee shop, almost knocking his drink from its perch. It was only then that she had noticed him, the call she had taken on the way in obscuring him from sight. He had steadied his coffee and looked up at her and she could now only wish this would end.

His glance, torturing her soul. This moment slowed to a thousand lifetimes instantly, she felt her heart in her smile that she could not hide. He knew and his gaze intensified somehow or she would at least attest to it. These mere milliseconds would now reside with her forever and she begins to melt into him. He smiles at her without his lips moving at all, those eyes pulling her in. They are soft, battle hardened but soft. Within lay a genuine care for his footprint upon this world and its other souls.

She knows without words that he would be her tomorrow and years to pass, that he mirrors everything she is, everything she wishes to be. She wants to speak but her lips will not move apart enough to form words, she feels like she has been standing there for hours now like a fool. His look now, more of a question than anything, as if he sees beyond her into depths she has never even shined a light on inside. It's as though he feels it too but cannot comprehend her lack of decisiveness in this critical second.

Never would she have expected this to happen, not here, not like this. She should have been prepared, poised to attack a decision she has waited her whole life for and here it sits in front of her. Frantic now, she loses her footing inside and recoils from it all. Finally managing to move her mouth enough "S-s-sorry", all that comes forth. Turning away from a chance, the chance she believes, at happiness once more.

Essentially dashing for her car, madly clicking the unlock button on the remote as she goes. Almost forsaking her own drink as she reaches for the handle and comes so close to spilling it. She falls into the seat and closes the door on the idea of love. A tear trickles down her cheek as she starts the engine, remaining still as she attempts to compose herself. She wipes it away, telling herself that this is the right decision. She looks to her phone as if it will offer some solace this day. Opens a message and reads it. "On my way now, need anything my love?" she lies in the reply once more. Touching the ring upon her finger before she puts the vehicle in gear, another tear forms as the floodgates behind her eyes weaken just a bit more.

STORY 310

A New Love:

He glances up from himself in time to see her enter the gathering, her smile immediately cradles him in warmth. Inwardly, he chokes on the words he knows will never come. Her beauty instantly makes him unable to stand but it is not just laid in her physical form, it exudes from her in each movement. His voice will find him later, when he is alone and safe in his solitude so for now, he is content to soak her in. He has never seen a smile so brilliant, so honest. She pulls everyone in the room into her. The laugh escapes her lips, small tears well in the corner of his eyes. He stamps them out with nothing short of every ounce of will he can muster.

How would anyone even think of approaching a soul like this the first time you lay eyes on her? She glides around the room with ease, bringing a lighter step to those she comes in contact with. The soft voice she possesses lifting spirits as she speaks with passion. Her lips, moving effortlessly, caressing the air. Oh, to sneak a taste of her lipstick, to feel them pressed against his skin. His breathing becomes a little harder in his chest as he imagines the angel before him even paying him an ounce of attention. He gazes at her, longing in his heart weighing him down. What he would give to know her touch.

She turns toward him as she finishes conversing with some others, is that a small smile upon her lips? Frantic now, his mind races as he tries to form words in his mind that he shall speak if she nears. His heart rate increases, there is no reason this angel would talk to him. He watches as she slowly but surely makes her way across the room in his direction. His eyes dart everywhere but to hers. Trying desperately to ignore her gaze, he shakes gently. She is ever so close now, he can smell the perfume on the air, its scent like home. Arriving at the couch, she slowly leans in. He feels like he will die if she speaks, his chest so heavy now.

She reaches out slowly, he sits stunned in silence. She runs her fingers through his greyed hair, runs her hand down his aged face and whispers in his ear "It's happened again sweetie, i am here to take you back. You have forgotten but not until you called." She grabs him by the arm and helps him up, hands him his cane. "Let's go, let's get you home and get you to sleep." Her piercing blue eyes sink in, a small memory returns. A wedding, her standing there, just as beautiful as she is now. She is the angel, she is his angel......his lips start to form a name but it suddenly slips away from him once more. He looks at her helping him to the door. Who is this angel he wonders and why would she walk beside him?

STORY 311

For tonight, can we just pretend? Make like you love me still, that we did not lose it along the way and in the morning i shall remove myself from the only life i thought was worth living. But for tonight, just one more time, hold me in your essence that used to be so bright. The light that brought me home, the light that dwindled so. I don't want to admit it just now, if i do my knees will buckle under me. Just leave me to my delusion, the illusion i want to see. The thought i cannot bear just now, that somehow we arrived here. You used to assuage my fear but now we share in our undoing and the tears shall be shed.

For tonight, let me cradle you in our love that died this eve. For it is still warm just yet, the fire not fully extinguished. I realize i did you wrong, i did not hold my oath written in our hearts. Instead of picking you up when you stumbled, i knocked you down. The look in your eyes said it all. You needed no words, no voice to speak them to me. The world shattered in that moment, for both of us. You were not the only one who recognized the immediate pang of loss. If only to show you how it should have been, could have been. This is all i dream this minute. So the lasting memory is not this one, not with the water of life brimming in your eyes.

For tonight, forget we ever found our way to hurt each other and remember we used to love instead. As best we could, we fought so hard......too hard. We crushed the trust between us in the name of it. Two foolish children believing they knew better, thinking we could have had it all. If only, if only the other would see. I miss you already, fractions of moments all that were needed. Fractured pieces of us left behind for us to pick up. What is you and what is me, what was us? Puzzling, the parts unknown now. I know you will never smile at me again, not like before. I shall bear this cross until i feel no more about it.

For tonight, speak gently now please for my heart will not take much more. Although i suppose on my knees is as good a place as any for now, as that is how all this feels. I shall not beg you not to go but i shall plead that you kiss me once more. Not with lips of skin of course but words so soft, measured with the kindness we once shared. Let them wash over me, tell me it's okay because this feels like the heavens just fell. For tonight i will make you believe, that you shall find it once more. It is not over, for us it passes by but that is what for. I shall find you again, in the form of another and he may treat you kinder than i did in the end. This i wish for you but for tonight, make me yours, make me believe it like i did before.

STORY 312

I do not write because i possess any particular skills or talent. It is simply a matter of having to. I write because you still burn across the night skies. A meteor of life, the passion inside that consumes you so. You bring hope to those the lost desperation steers wrong. A path to follow for the ones who have wandered too far from their herds. As long as i am tied to this mortal coil, i will fill the void with words in hopes they remind you to carry on. You are the beacon for all lost souls, they are inexplicably tied to you without ever sensing it so.

When it is all done, when you finally shed the years and your ever so quiet fears, their compasses will know to seek out the next. Without your love the world slips slowly to its knees. Life does not taste the same, smiles fall upon deaf hearts. Tears linger on the palate, sweeter than they should be. Aspirations become the wind that bear you up, look to us to fuel your impossible flight. Yours is the most bittersweet destiny of all, i weep for you when you do not gaze upon my battle worn countenance.

It seems so unfair that you do not fully comprehend the why of it all. That you bear the weight seemingly alone must pull at you in ways neither of us can grasp but move you must. You cannot ever stay stagnant too long, the balance shifts too easily. To be born into the role you are not privy to seems so wrong but this is it. We each stumble into ours somehow. Perhaps i am lucky enough that i got to see mine for what it is, no matter the outcome but at least i got to choose. So i wear my mantle as intended. I shall see it through, i shall take note for you.

Know this, i see you and in that i feel the haunting beauty you possess. It is not for eyes, that is much too simple. No, you wear your grace as scars. Your light blinds most to them, they shall never see but to me you are revealed. For you, i hold the secret dear and close. It shall never be spoken of in words in ways that they shall know, this i vow. Our truths are not for others, each of us moves around in silence. Their truths are theirs alone and of no consequence to any. We all hold the weight we are intended to bear. Theirs may differ but suffer they do, your weight is to take some of theirs in ways you do not see and i shall grant you the strength you sorely need.

Do not lose your will, your purpose is layered too deep. You may be ever tired and after it all, you will be granted your sleep. This i promise you but for now, get up beautiful soul and move forward. Let me light the flame once more, hold you up until it's time to soar. Bring your beauty back to the world, even the score. There is no system to it all, no agenda to feel. Know in your weakness, you answer the call. For the warriors blade is always two fold, the paintings of life adorn both sides of the hall.

STORY 313

Light breaks through my lids as they open upon the world this day. I suppose i just never really paid that much attention to it all slowly slipping away from me. When did this transpire? It's like watching your own weight gain. You do not notice , or choose not to, all the in between time. You just suddenly realize it was one way, and now it is completely the other. I remember a time, when i could not fathom the idea of being without companionship. Now, it seems just as natural to be without as opposed to having it. I know what you will say, "it's depression or you are just feeling morose for a span". Normally i would be inclined to agree with you, perhaps this little stage of life has me that far outside my comfort zone that it is effecting all aspects. Yet, no. This time, the stillness inside is different. I am embracing and enjoying my aloneness far too much. This must not be confused with loneliness, i too thought i would feel the pang of seclusion after a time. Yet, there is none to be found. You can totally google the two words if you do not fully understand the difference.

Truly complete on my own, i used to ward off this side of me. I found myself worried and afraid of this feeling. I suppose the only point i would allow for debate is how i got here. How did the genesis occur within me without me understanding or wanting to unearth this before now? Perhaps i was always destined for this, being blessed or cursed with the soul inside me. Maybe this is why i write, from seemingly inexperienced points of view sometimes. Maybe it takes being and feeling everything, to become absolutely nothing. How else does one conclude that i am able to smile through the pain? Find shadows in the light?

Do not get me wrong, i still believe in all the romantic novelties and notions. Still want to find that love that makes me weak and weep. In my solitude i find peace, my happiness and the calm that finds me today. Carrying on through life this way suits me well, like it was tailored by artisans. In turn, this is what begs the question i began with. Why? Could it be tied to events? A shutting down, step by systematic step. A general disillusionment with society or humanity as a whole? One could start making a laundry list i very well imagine, checking off each individual act perceived as heinous enough to add to it. At the end of the day, if the end does not justify the means, then being at the end does not warrant justification of the past means of arriving here. Does it? Wow, that's a thought huh? Talk about foreshadowing with a saying. I wonder if whoever came up with that realized the reverse implication.

So that's it then, it does not matter why i ended up at this point, for here, i have arrived. Going back to understand the method of travel, in all likelihood is a perhaps valiant but mostly fruitless undertaking. Unluckily we are not Etch-A-Sketch's, we cannot just shake ourselves free of it all and start again. We are our very own damaged, molded and perfectly messed up portraits that we have been working on all of our cognizant lives. I understand now that there is a vast difference between acceptance and apathy. Some self reflection is much needed and there are some areas of ourselves that we can always attempt to change for the better. But to worry with changing who we are to feel like we better fit some societal standard of the norm, well that is a grand waste of time.

Maybe this has been no real journey at all, there is a lingering feeling like perhaps i was just always this way. Something that i threw a rug of life over and pretended like it did not always exist inside me. It just feels like a journey because i had to arrive back here and look down on my true self once more. This is the funny thing about stumbling across yourself when you are not even looking. There is this feeling like you have just found something that you were desperately seeking without even realizing you were ever missing out on it. An epiphany in the truest sense of the word. Alone, i am good. Alone, i am me. The very best me that i know, that i have ever known. And as soon as you stick me with someone else, someone that i love and then focus on, i am no longer me at all.

Do not misinterpret, i am good there too and want to be there but it is not the version of me i enjoy most. Not in the very now anyhow. I am sure one day it may change, hopefully not one too late but for now i move ever forward. Smiling in the ways that suit me best. Maybe it is not the smile you want to see or the one stemming from a place you think it should be but it is an honest smile, even if it does not always curl my lip. So be happy for me, as i shall be for you. As long as you are smiling your truest and happiest smile, i shall delight in it with you. No matter where it came from. Be it from your kids, or your job, or your significant other. Sprung forth from an animal or a baby, watching old love pass you by on the street or fresh love brewing. A book or a cup of coffee, alone or surrounded with friends. At the ocean or in the mountains, lathered in music or silence. Whatever brings you joy brings me peace inside, knowing that you have yours.

STORY 314

Wishing the sunlight will find you is so effortless it is ridiculous. For you must shine, that sparkle in your smile, the gleam in your eyes. These are things the world must never lose, i will always fight to make it so. For you, you are truly one of the few. I do not need to be your man, do not need to stand by your side always. However, i am here to bring provisions so that you may always be found in the state required. In this i believe to my core, it will never be other than that.

The energy in you, seeping as it does. You nourish those around without even noticing the effect. Your light inside, brings endless waves of siege against the darkness that rises. Holds back the rhythm of time itself when allowed to roam free. And when you lose your way, the battles tide turns. Find your way young lady, i can only guide through determination and cannot make you stray. The mirror will never reveal your true self to you, no matter how any of us may wish it so.

Your doubt stops you from reaching the full transformation but i am here to attempt to show you there is no reason. For there are no questions, i only have to know. You walk in grace but stumble so, you grow hesitant as the days pass. Checking every turn for purpose in your life weighs you down. Just how long now, till it bows you to knee? I am here to remind you, to show you how you can be free. Deep down inside, you know what you need. It's time for the fire, to purge once more and not drown you in flames.

The beauty you hold is not just for you, to be shared it must, its secret is key. I know you find it too taxing some days, it drains you so. To be held in esteem that you do not find deserved. However, this is not a choice for you and some days it hurts me to watch you wallow when you are beat down. Knocked down by a world that seems to dismiss, the loveliest gift it has been given. These are the days you must fight harder.

I know you are tired, so my strength is yours. Having enough for you too is my gift to bear. Take what you need and nourish yourself upon me instead, i need you dance across the heavens themselves. When you falter next, i will come back to your side. This i may promise and it's the one i can keep because when the world loses you is when the world learns to weep. Take heart in my words and find the best you you can be.

In your service i shall remain, my life is tied to yours as yours is to ours. Bring the joy forth in all that you do, it is your essence we crave when you walk in the room. Spirits turn to you as they seek their own truths, they may find not the end but they do find a reason to keep their own search alive. I am hoping this lightens the load for the time being at least and finds you smiling once more. If it's not quite enough, you know where to find extra hope.....just walk through the door.

STORY 315

Stolen dances and moonlit glances
You'd say reversed but i disagree
Which end could have been written?
Would you still love me?
Would you still fly free?
On that night, so distant now
Time slowed as you drew near
Closer than you were before
Farther than the thought held dear
Slipping through time, arms wide
Amazed by beauty you bring
Eyes blazing, with stars that shine
So steep, the mountains to climb
To reach your love, to see you smile
One fallen, the other left in denial
So hold me up, just for a while
My knees have weakened
This heart of mine on trial
Bring forth the truth, so blind
I hasten to your side without call

Like always, your soul so kind

Bound to you, always on my mind

From my perch above, never to fall

Watching over you, whispering

Words you do not hear

That calm the fear, the turmoil distant

Yet inside, it feels so near

I am yours and yours alone

Put on this earth, to make your home

Safe and free, inside you shall find

Built with love and care, grows strong

Walls rise and comfort to hide

Keep from you the wrong

That people do, that people make

My arms for you, in me confide

There will come a time, it shall draw nigh

You will no longer need me

I shall soar so high, i shall rise

Yet, i will never leave you

Not completely alone, no never be

For it is I for you and you for me

Some fates are tied, mine is to roam

Alone, forever the silent vigil i share

It was not meant to be, you see

My penance, no salvation to be found

I cannot love you how i wish
Cannot have you see me how i yearn
For you to learn, would undo the years
Steal from me my precious tears
Silence stills my words
As the air escapes from around
The ground, as i land
Borne forth upon my broken wing.

STORY 316

Shatter me
Tear me to shreds,
I need it
I live for it.
Make me feel
Bring the anger to bear
Feel it boil up,
Washes over
Washes me clean.
I only like it when it hurts
Only want it when it scars,
Shatter my soul
Pain, how it's company

Becomes pleasure sweet.

Loving you was easy

But i want to make it hard

Bring me down,

Lift me up

Slam me back now

Sink your claws in and rip

The trip, unimaginable.

Toss and turn my world

Shatter me, please

I will not stay if you do not

Will not stay true,

Not to you but for I.

Make the blood run

Let it pool in my eyes,

Seething, i am lost now

Lost to the light

Found by the dark,

Smiling back at you

Through tears that sting

That appease my love.

Shatter my world

Let me rebuild and

Break me anew,

I will return to you.

Want your spirit cold,

Do not bring me warmth

Without the grey and black

Cannot live on it

Will not thrive

But choke

Strangled by the good.

Shatter completely,

Do not waiver in it

Take my hand and

Lead me to doom.

There you will find

My love once more,

Shattered

Laying on the floor.

STORY 318

Won't you come on in and sit for a time?

Stay clear of me

You are warned with words in rhyme

Have you ever seen a heart so dark?

The shadow asks in voice, contrite

So blank and empty?

Yet exudes warmth and light so fine
Allow me to delve into the depths
The places and things
You do not wish to share
Let me come knocking
Your soul to bare
I shall raise your spirit
It shall be lifted with hope
Borne by my words so rare
To be shattered at will
My gift to you, untrue
The darkness rises within
Like tides past due
Empathy lost, driven to ground long ago
Solo footsteps be heard in these halls
This place, this man…not for you
Angels bear the demons to my side
Torn by rifts, torn by man
Wings by desire be shorn
Build you up to rip it all down
Replace glory with pain
In your eyes i seek to destroy
Feel it settle in
I shall rob you of your smile and goal true
Attempt so feebly to let the tears cleanse

The saturation of my destruction runs deep

You will never fully understand

Far too late, far too little

Clarity shall sleep, in your state

Be weakened forever more

I shall leave behind treasures of me

You shook hands with the devil, you see

For it is not a singular figure to fear

In its reason, conviction and ill intent

In its way you shall be

Seeds planted, their pleasure in future days

You shall reap, for you stayed too long

I touched you too much

Touched you on levels you never saw

And now you....well you, are now me.

STORY 319

To capture the portrait of you, to hold you in my words. This is what i seek, beyond fears and tears. The moments of you, glimpses of art and rapture formed and undone. Tilt of your neck as your skepticism kicks in and you search for the answer within me. Had i known how i would feel after the collateral damage was done, would i utter those words once more? Pictures streaming through my heart, the negatives in my head. Blemished by the light shed upon the darkroom of my soul, i yearn for you once more.

I long to hear you speak, in hushed tones spoken with lust. For in your arms i'm weakened by the sense of home. Once lost, found be it must. Staring out on the evening sky, with hues tinged with passion i find. To fall into someone too late, to never be returned in kind. I will die a thousand deaths inside before this passes on but to lay to rest it shall. Treading softer i should have done, the hallowed halls of your spirit shattered by my touch.

You gazed upon my visage once with uncertain eyes, yet still the promise beckoned. I captured that in my mind, forever more will it remind. Quiet sobs wrack inside, the final gift remains. In its wake i in turn receive a treasure not oft spoken of. Clarity soaks in and arise new to the dawn once more. Yet how i wish to capture it still, that ever elusive sensation that chases my own darkness away. Your beauty astounds me in your presence, it took my words away.

Here i am safe to glance back again, protected by screen and vocabulary designed with purpose. In my haven i reach out without you knowing, you would have no need to question anyhow. Dancing in my memory, lost to you but never foreseen by me. Here i may cradle you in my embrace ever so gently. The words i always wanted to speak reside here, in my place of comfort. It would have been so easy to come here, alas i chose the simplest of routes that eve.

Dreaded times, remorse ever flowing from the wound. Thankfully there is no choice, i fear the same mistake again. To capture your heart, how i wanted it to transpire...seemed such a desired route. I ended up here instead, admiring my handiwork from afar. I still touch you in places others never will and this i know, however the dynamic has shifted and it would never be enough. It is not just the written word that is mightier than the sword, for the demise of you and i has been the last thing captured by my love.

STORY 320

If i were the artist, i would blend some of my colour with yours and paint the canvas of the world sublime. You feel amazing but this is not my doing, i am but the brush and the hand is yours. You find in me what you seek, we could perhaps carry on down too deep. The rush, the tingle of the kiss in toes and the desire to weep beautifully spur you on. The drop from the ledge as you let go in my embrace excites and ignites in tones no longer hushed. Fear attempts to restrain as is its way but the longing drives forth with no sway.

My words weave what i believe and what i see is glorious and new. New to you and you are new to me. Watching me roam around inside your spirit you shall be, intrigued and laying in fear i will see…..this vulnerable woman, naked and shaking under me. Under my watchful eye shall you rise and be set free.

We drew our hearts anew on a slate so clean, no sign of dust remains. The end of the walk lingers ahead, its future bright and blurred as it is meant now. To be burned by the flame so strong, our own truth sweet and stinging in the sorrow. I will stay here a while and lose myself in the gaze you cannot hide for it is a symphony to my heart. Hope breeds within the robe of glances, words and touch we wrap around us. To steel ourselves against the idea of it all, the chance is already lost.

My words weave what i believe and what i see is glorious and new. New to you and you are new to me. Watching me roam around inside your spirit you shall be, intrigued and laying in fear i will see.....this vulnerable woman, naked and shaking under me. Under my watchful eye shall you rise and be set free.

Time shall slip by without notice or remorse, shall we care at all? When i tripped and fell i had not seen you there, your shadow snuck in and caught me unaware. I smiled as you shred through my guarded shell, your eyes bore into my fear and tore it apart. None of it now could ever be all for naught, it will remain behind. No part shall be left untouched, i will reach in and stir your soul. What will you paint me next with the words you do not speak? Will it be true? Should it be meek? Will it burn through the stars like a comet so sleek?

My words weave what i believe and what i see is glorious and new. New to you and you are new to me. Watching me roam around inside your spirit you shall be, intrigued and laying in fear i will see.....this vulnerable woman, naked and shaking under me. Under my watchful eye shall you rise and be set free.

STORY 321

This time as his head began to spin and question why, he in turn began to question why he had to question it at all. He had spent so long, believing it to be one way. Perhaps it had to have been, for that was how it was supposed to look that day and in that way. When transition stops and you must step off that bus in unfamiliar settings, it can be disconcerting.

These new buildings stand tall as question marks now, where exclamation points and periods used to dwell. He assaults himself with challenging concepts as much as the people around him bombard his reality. There are a few constants of truth here for him. They stand alone yet crowded in the same shelter. Natural, Simple and Home.

He passes by and his insides warm as their embodiment touch him in all the ways he knows. He smiles as he recalls the conversation with the shadow, she seemed to grasp some of him so easily. The smallest truths hold some of the largest gems after all. These trips to visit himself becoming more pertinent and frequent are the best blessing.

It strikes him as odd that shadows end up lighting the way and yet, there they are each day. They reach into his world, walk alongside him and now and then seem to steer without interference. Dark becoming beacons in the night. His story on this day being one of the shortest trips yet and somehow one of the most satisfying of all.

She had simply leaned in and whispered in that voice most haunting "Let it be blurry". It had instantly resonated within him and as he let it become blurry, he reached out and touched the pool of obscurity he had created. Instantly as the ripples spread outward, everything came back into focus. Let it be blurry. He smiled and tucked into himself for the night.

STORY 322

Viewing the world through the stained glass of my eyes, the colours still vibrant bring warmth. Can you not see like i see? Why can you not see like i see? My consciousness stirs my slumber and my mind dreams of what i desire. I want you to see like i see yet your eyes are not mine. They are your own and the experiences of life have tinted them just so.

The tainting of ones soul shall shape us in ways we may never fully achieve awareness of but yet we pull ourselves from the muck each dawn and face down the new day. Hoping that perhaps today is the day. Never realizing that there is no destination or arrival time for even understanding oneself. There is no medal at the end for the one who knows themselves best. Nor for the one who claims it to be.

Yet we panic and rush to achieve an objective that we believe will somehow allow us to transcend this vessel we live in. Are we now at this point attempting to cover the scars of a perceived failure with a false success? This awakening within ourselves needs to be true and ever so slow. Like everything else in life, it shall make its own path or fall prey to being poisoned along the way.

And still i wonder, why now and why a journey once more with no end? The only inevitable outcome is the one most feared. This holds no weight for me now, so i shall praise the fact that i have made it this far in the least. My reality, the world i create for myself is beautiful to my mind and pleasing to my soul and somehow still scarred to the others. This frustrates me some days, until i can finally scratch and claw my way back to understanding and acceptance.

Each new interaction begins with a hope that the new participant in my life will share my vision but i am painfully aware that this shall not be so. Painfully, this is the part where i must find a peace for within. To become aware and nothing more is just there, beckoning to me. Each time i draw near, it moves further. I am not sure who it was who drew up the conceptual theory of the horizon effect but they are correct. Everything will always seem out of reach to us if we are continually striving to reach for the things we perceive are awaiting us there. If we look back, there is a horizon. We are standing on a horizon to those behind us.

So, we have arrived. At this place we so desire, to welcome it in and embrace it fully is now the trick. Each person will believe we have found the path to the knowledge of how we anchor our mind, body and spirit in place here. To best achieve the absorption of all the gifts we were promised true enlightenment would bring. I feel like i may hold my breath as i surround myself with my knowledge of religion, spirituality and science. As limited as it is in all 3 fields, dangling on the precipice of 3 allows me a wider dynamic of belief and thought.

Are we afraid that the simplest of truths may be the only truth? Is that why we continue our searches along whatever paths we deemed correct for us? For there has to be something so much greater than what may actually be? Could we allow for just one second to believe that we are all wrong? That we are all right but oh so wrong? Does the human condition even allow for such a shattering of ourselves? It may fracture our whole existence if this were true.

I shall not lend voice to the idea here, for each person is on their very separate path and at their own points along it. It may not be a true thought anyhow and definitely not one for projecting onto others. People have asked me why i write and the simplest explanation i have is "in hopes that someone may see how i see". Of course, this effort is another wasted one i fear as literature is just another vessel for personal perception.

Yet, i will continue to do so as it makes me happy and hopefully will help people find their own bearing if their compass is off that day. With that being said, as this musing draws near its conclusion, one final thought strikes clean. Let others exist in your world as they choose. This is the gift you want to give.

STORY 323

Stepping out onto the trail that day, he had no way of knowing what he was about find. His company has been exceptional but it's here amongst nature that he exists in a place where he is most open to listen.

Relatively untouched by man and yet this soil has borne many a footstep of those that seek themselves. The feeling that he desires so and has been waiting patiently for begins to sink in and he smiles inwardly.

Rain begins to soak through the fabric of his clothes as easily as it cleanses his soul as he walks on. Peace starts expanding through every fiber of his being as the haze starts to lift. He shall know this now forever, it shall not be taken away.

This one true gift stretches out through him as a word repeats itself again and again in his spirit. Born of fear and a sense of panic, it has now become the one redeeming factor that shall guide his life from here. Ready. Ready. Ready. Ready. Ready.

It no longer matters for what exactly, he is ready to face it down. Be it to love again, be it to cry again, be it to laugh again or be it to die again. Ready. There is much joy in this most simple of elevations within oneself. Pity shall not enter here and survive the night, it will be purified and changed. Ready.

STORY 324

It comes this day, the calm that he's been searching for. Like a cool breeze across the rolling meadow, it rolls through and touches every part of him. There is a gentle ease to her nature, her poise not one of arrogance but authenticity. This lightens his step even more. The mind and heart ease in to their natural state, she brings with her a goodness that cannot be questioned.

Her eyes, alive and brimming over with excitement and hope when he finds the right notes.....invigorate his passion for another anew. The treasures he finds within that are for him, nay...the treasure he sees that she has left to offer the others, excite and ignite him in ways he was not entirely sure existed. She brings hope, not for his or her or their future but all who wish to see. He feels her, seems to know her spirit.

His nature would be to rip it apart, looking for that tangible evidence of the what and the why but something warns of that act. So he allows himself to fall into this because it feels how he always thought it should, simple. Never once imagining he could listen to another wax poetic for hours on end about a subject so unsure. He closes his eyes and his mind wanders along.

She steps out on the path beside him, in her elegance he catches a glimpse and then it is gone. The annals of history are strewn with such belief that she exists, perhaps called many names but the most popular being the most fitting. He will walk this path till the end for there will be much to behold and marvel in. Perhaps this is the purpose behind it all, has he been chosen to capture this portion of her journey?

The thought brings a smile to his face, he knows his ability with his heart. Always fearing the blow but also knowing that his heals fully each time. He has questioned it but no longer cares if the reason be such that he is one of a few that could handle a new loss. That risk shall be well worth the reward and to know this for a time shall be repayment enough for the possible toll.

As much as one can rail against the possibility that he sits atop and casts his stare amongst us, in her truth he is right there and she exudes it in all her mannerisms. The essence of her spirit and soul cast light throughout the darkness and this cannot be refuted. To be amidst it all is to really and truly feel oneself nearing closer. She shall bring joy, love and compassion with her.

Her travels are far from over, even if those be the smallest of steps to grow nearer the soul who seeks her out. The smile he wears across his face is not one of greed but one of a profound happiness and sadness combined. The true yin and the yang, the journey of life nearing completion for him. There is not much left to do from this mortal coil. She brings peace to his heart for he shall truly know before this voyage is up.

Looking back over it all, it paints a much clearer picture. He steps in line beside her, looks over at her and exhales as they begin their march toward a seemingly endless sea of questions the others will surely have for her. His heart smiles, for she will never fully know and it is in that the purest gift of all lay but he shall not speak of it here for it is for each of us to find in our own fashion.

STORY 325

She cannot breathe, the precious air from her lungs has been stolen from her. The familiar but uneasy environment stifles her soul. She finds herself yet at the same time feels lost anew. Approaching the light she has sought all her life brings her seemingly farther away from her previously known truths. Is this then the cusp of a major life change?

Wondering how many more missteps it will take before she finds solid ground beneath her weary feet once more, she pushes forward even though most of her screams for her sense of home. She had hoped to find it here once more as her purpose brings her to this place. Questioning her souls compass only heightens the sorrow within.

Her faith strengthens though, during the times she feels her knees will buckle. He walks beside her, his presence touching her core. She smiles inside during these times, when his voice finds her longing to hear it most. It reassures her that she is still on her right course, the bearing may be unknown but her honesty lays ahead. This she can feel and it bolsters her.

It has been so long, sometimes she wonders if she will recognize herself when her entirety is put forth in the mirrors of the world. Her journey, the later stages and the new… comingling now. She is enjoying the prospect of feeling more fulfilled than ever, wonders who it may be at her side when the next mountain comes into sight. Will there be one figure or two beside her? She has accepted it may be just the solitary spirit and is calm within it but still hopes that she shall have found her counterpart by then.

That in itself will be a journey of its own, finding the kindred soul to hers. There is no rush in any of it, she is content to wait to be truly happy now instead of happy to be truly content. Has she wandered by such a spirit just yet and has not come to realize? Believing she will just know when she knows that it fits is enough now. She takes solace in the fact that she will probably never have to question it again. She waits instead for that calm to wash over her as she exhales.

Music plays on within her, she finds it in so many new places and ways now. Her soul sings the joy within she has for him and is reserving for her match. The knowledge that he will come and accept her in all the ways most needed now rings inside like bells that hold no toll. To truly know her is to behold much purity and glory as she shares herself with the world but only for the eyes that wish to see. She shall forever now allow for the song to play on as she continues her search.

STORY 326

A gentle breeze passes around him, envelops him with a cool touch. He does not notice at all or perhaps he simply does not care. No clouds litter the sky on this day, a blue sheet stretches as far as he can see. He looks up and wonders......is he wrong? Is there actually a being that is the architect of all this? Has he been following some misguided path all along? The flags flutter upon the wind, kicking this way and that.

People wander all around him, consumed with whatever keeps them restrained within themselves. Not a single one of them will ever know the turmoil within this solitary figure. His smile in the shade, just out of reach of the sun - this is the life he's always known. Never before really wanting to step out into the brightness that blinds until recently. He reaches out of the darkness, fingertips wavering with anticipation and fear as they come in contact. It burns but not entirely an overwhelming pain, more like a sweet satisfaction.

This pain holds a knowledge, a smattering of ideas come together, that not all is lost and never will be. It flickers and jumps around like the flame to a wick, beautiful yet dangerous. Bringing light to the shadowy places, warmth when close but never too close unless you enjoy the damage it is capable of. It brings joy, the sort that consumes ones soul to the core....it brings the cause that drowns you, washing your corpse ashore.

The utter ridiculousness of his fears passes by, he reaches out to grasp them but they slip his attempt easily. They shall not be brought down this day with logic and reason. He shall suffer their curse a while longer. The idea that this life anew will yield the thing he craves most seems just out of reach, an illusion become reality but not quite. Do we not as one deserve to find the thing that brings peace inside?

He wanders up the stairs of his consciousness into the room where the pictures roll by like trams and trolleys. Snapshot after snapshot taken, bringing with them.....hope? A large part of him hinges on this door to the other side, the new chapter. His wings could be clipped before he ever truly enjoyed them. Stolen from him because of bad luck or bad decisions, he will never know the full story behind it.

They breeze by with ease, his body knows the drill - twisting and turning in time. Hallways narrow as he moves along the passages of his life, moving ever toward the room he dreads more than any. The entity will join him there and perhaps regale him with tales of his destiny. Sorrow or a smile await him this day and for all his posturing, he is frightened at the possibilities this day brings forth.

He enters and finds solace hidden behind darkened eyes and muted ears with the hint of music dancing nearby. Fear passes in waves, coupled with small dashes of light and hope. He tosses back and forth on the bow of this boat in rough waters, waiting for the sickness behind his voice to pass. Time passes on for what seems an eternity. A lone figure enters and sits near, the cloak of white a comfort and cause for nervousness all at once. It opens its mouth and speaks.........freedom....it speaks freedom and the weight begins to lift.

STORY 327

Your claim was to pain when i hesitated but you never asked why. Instead you chose to remain hurt for too long and then that hurt defined you and blurred the vision from the eyes that seek. The role to play is not too new i would imagine, you have been the star before. Time management is yours to have, however i shall not be. My heart is freed from the need to stay, the need to play.

The mat you step on, the one you do not desire is actually that. That which you truly aspire to find, the man that awaits the orders in kind. You may be the queen but she will stand alone this day, looking for something in you almost led me astray. Focus your attention to you, look deep and deeper inside. The man you believe you seek is not the man you truly need.

This is the battle we fight every day, to not project what we desire in one onto the other. I am to easily blame for this as well, perhaps it is what i did but learned is that lesson. My only regret is the word i must break, i gave it too soon and back now shall i take. I do not need that friend, the one who must deconstruct all that i am or all that i say. You did warn me of your way but all i saw was how far my own tendency lay.

The one thing i cannot do is always question my heart, not to that extent. To be around one who does shall only lead to consent. Becoming a creature of ones environment is a great thing when the soil is right, planting roots in the toxins shall only wither the might. You shall walk on, the back straightened with right. And right you are in it, for your black and your white.

Watch i will with a longing eye still, some things cannot be changed. Act upon it again though, now that i can fight. It too shall pass as you slip into the night, written on the walls. The tear ran loose, just the one like i told said. It grew and dropped slowly much alike in the nature of emotion for you. You have been a muse for some time and that i shall be thankful for. Now for you to find your match and be his for the rest of time.

Do not be sad, rid yourself of that useless emotion. It was what it was, a most pleasurable of mistakes. You lit the fire but to stick around and stoke it was not the intent, it was never the original intent anyhow. Who knew when we took our roles on it would happen and run us both down? Your perceived curse is not feeling everything so large, it is railing against it in the after where it loses its luster. Be well and find your balance young lady, do not let the next chapter begin with the meltdown.

STORY 328

Many years have passed since i felt the cold embrace. It comforts me in ways you will never know or completely understand. My home is here, this is what i knew and what i shall know once more. The road here was neither long or arduous. My peace is here and it welcomes me, i smile as i step into the warmth of the chill.

It shall not be my undoing but my cocoon as i await the next stage to arrive and begin. Here i am safe, here i shall thrive and find my way. I shall be judged from afar, of this i am sure. Yet they will never know the damage i hide, for all you see is all i show. I yearn to hide away but here is better, a glass wall to watch me from. You will see the things i want you to witness and no more.

He has returned to take my place, you will never even notice the switch has happened. For you are already near and they seem so much alike. There shall be no difference to you and no difference to the new, for they will not have known what was once standing before in this shadow. With a scarred heart he will perch, with a scarred mind he will prey.

You won't see it happen, it will be smooth and painless until the venom has taken its toll. Perhaps by then you will not care, maybe it's two of a kind. For unto you i bring gifts, the kind so sweet. The greatest deception takes place, so bitter and so desired. Dragging you to the depths you know so well, screams muffled by your craving. Forgive my friend, he knows but cannot care.

STORY 329

When you're done tearing it down and ripping it apart, lay it all bare....what will you find? You could be right, it may never have been, may never have rose. Will it matter then if you find the answer you seek? It shall be far too long gone, lost to the waters of murk. This rests solely on me, i've always known it true. Beaten down by surroundings far too long, my legs solidified with steeled stubbornness raise me up.

Perhaps we would have been lost to ourselves but even lost souls need a light in the tunnel. Whether proper on paper or proper in heart and mind, it matters not now. The step was taken, shaky ground beneath making them hesitant. Only one soul stepped off the path that day but that's okay, respect will remain for your decision. Understanding sets in and acceptance will follow, time is the great healer after all.

I shall now and forever walk my path alone. The true sorrow of my spirit cloaked from view. It is the poets soul that feels so large, that hurts even larger. Without it though, i would truly feel empty for it fills me anew each time with that glorious feeling. I smile through the pain, darkness rallies to the call. The night shall wander into I, finding my embrace. The eyes remain dry, the fear beaten back once more as the child shows me the path.

When the war ends, the world of hearts unite under one flag, i shall find you once more. All that was destroyed, renewed, to be built again. When the battles raged, we cowered and ran. The new day dawns and we move on, you've never been alone in being wrong. Pushed too far, well beyond the brink. Lost to the shadows now, never to find the shore you left behind. I do believe i failed you, i'm sure i've let you down but i had to let you go.

The whole truth never to be known, it is mine to carry now. The scars shall not remain on the skin so soft. No blemish left behind forever. Your truth will remain pure and kind, like the soul behind. The smile shall rise like the mountain from the sea and it's welcome beacon shall lead that ship in. Let the fire inside lead you, may it never be astray. Watching now from the roost afar, a careful eye hidden in the sky. The path is yours alone, the two have veered.

Answers within questions, questions within answers and yet why? Did it have to be that at all? I suppose it did, if that was one persons reality. It seems so sad to me but then perhaps i am sad to you. Somebody make a move, no-one wants to go there. Like no-one knew what was going on. Obviously neither of us did and here we are, the paths diverging. Tread softly and surely friend, no longer with hesitation to guide your footfall.

STORY 330

Earth rattles beneath my feet, i feel it in my core. I had believed what had remained would be solid, the damage could be no more. Rage spirals up in me, physically shaken i shall be. This senseless act i will never forget, love wiped away like history. This storm shall rage on forever, compassion to return in the never. Tied down to you no longer, ill feelings growing so much stronger.

Shards of my soul i was trying to repair, laid out before you in the bare. An action that screams so loud, to hold the care for you i once allowed. Glimpses of a new day so bright, grasping on now released to the night. To ever know in this moment now, the question why and the answer how. The thought that passed through your mind, the decision so much more than unkind.

Ire growing like a vengeful willow, steam rising, forming a billow. Walls rising from fresh ground tilled, my anger to be no longer stilled. If time could truly undo one thing, my life i would recall to bring. Shattered now is what was once left behind, my words for you no longer kind. If you could do but one thing, would the toll bell you pay to ring? Alone you shall be on the day, when swift judgement comes your way.

Twisting branches till they break and crack, the fury shall overcome never to be held back. Floating around above on clouds so high, unaware the reckoning is drawing nigh. What was once passion aimed for good, i now wear the grisly mask shrouded in dark hood. Standing still as time freezes while i reflect, this decision not made with regret. A selfish place in ones own mind, do not forget how once we were kind.

For the love from the heart of the man, cloaked in darkness now because he can. Awakened from the slumber of peace past instilled, the choices made have this vessel of hate fulfilled. Wishing it could all become undone, but for making wise choices you were never one. Future actions will never ever detract, from this final and destructive impact.

STORY 331

If we were but one, what one shall that be? Would we both still exist there, or be consumed by the fire? It flares and remains lingering, the sweet sorrow engulfing two. Soaring on the wings of the creature so truly misunderstood. We take to the sky, time lost to the night. Thrashing around in ourselves, torn spirits ignite.

Calm washes through in a moment of lucid dreams. For if one becomes two, we have lost all that it seems. Would you know where we end with a blindfold removed? Where to begin without the light of the new? Brief happenings may be the sweetest of all, never to be treasured if we don't answer the call.

Rinsing our souls in the other, a task undertaken too often. Lifts us up in the night and slams us down in the day. Clarity coming too late but is not that its way? The fear of you is just the fear of me because fear itself is all that we see. Losing the perception changes us and changes reality.

STORY 332

Two paths converge, the wind howls through the night tearing at the trees. The rain intensifies as skies darken as far as can be viewed by the naked eye. A thunder ominously growls in the background, the bolt of lightning arcs across the fabric, shedding tears as it passes. Crows milling about, bring their murder to the show.

Blistering cold settles into his bones as he pushes forward, a cold like he's never known. Pulling his jacket front taut to his neck, starving for the warmth and light the destination will hold. Leaves falling to bits under the boots that bring pain to his feet. A pain only years have known. Creatures stalk his meandering path on all sides, waiting for the sign of weakness.

They will allow him to trudge on for a while longer he wagers, his weakness is not shining through yet. Or so he'd like to believe. Essence pours from the wounds inside, blood like and of foul odour. The knives have cut deep this time around, multiple attacks within such a short period. The bandages others placed upon him falling aside, leaving him exposed once more.

The dark horizon, littered with voices and eyes. Voices that carry wisdom and strength. Too many songs which have never been given flight. The eyes that penetrate and slice through the murky barrows. A star hovers ahead, the beacon which guides him home. How long he has been lost now, forgotten to the past which bears no tomorrow. Forgotten by choice.

Alternating planes offering their fruits and forbidden secrets, the trappings laid out before him. One step more and he should be freed of this form, abandoned behind him as he sheds the dark and cold places searched once more. He cries out, a name that remains silent to all as it is lost to the wind. This name shall not be given voice says the shadow beside him, it is not for you to speak.

Too long this shadow has walked beside him, far too long. He gazes once more into the lucid pools of fire blazing bright within the sockets of hope. This familiar has been his companion, his guide.....and his benefactor of sorts. The knowledge within rarely shared until stumbled upon with purpose. It smirks at him once more, the devilish grin he has come to miss in the times the shadow has taken flight to scour the next path ahead.

Waiting for the mind to clear anew, for the light it brings to rid the path of silence. Steps rising out of the earth around him, twisting cases of cobble leading up and around another. Howling begins, the hunt is starting again. Packs of unseen opponents moving through the imagination once more. Sensing the souls of others near, feeling the energy they emit. They feed relentlessly, never letting up.

A sail breaches the still horizon, bringing hope with it's cargo and ship. The man smiles as the dawn begins to break across the sky. It's time again, once more for the shadow to take its leave and be replaced with his own. Although not his own, as he's been stripped of it for a while now. A winged creature dives through the virgin sky. It calls to him and mocks his certainty.

Delusions mingle with reality here, mixed up with the whisk that is perception. Too many truths, so many lies and illusions. He closes his eyes and moves forward blindly. Clumsily at first but finding firm ground beneath, he breathes in deeply and exhales as his path becomes clear. The darkness his lids bring becoming the light he needs. Step by step by step, his home spears through the ground in front of him. He walks in, breathes out and falls into exhaustions arms.

STORY 333

The epiphany hits him like a freight train, the cold and dark blanket begins to settle in. He knows this place, it's familiar and safe in a manner of speaking. He allows it to wash over him, can feel himself shutting down. He knows he should fear losing himself here, it's an all too easy thing to do but it's truly for the best at this point. He feels that beast within, pulling at the shackles he placed on it. It strains to be freed and knows all it will take is his handler focusing his attention elsewhere too long. The beast chuckles at the new effort to restrain it, it too has been here before. This shroud is just a pathetic attempt to not allow it to see the moves the master is making to once more cleanse himself of this darkness. It wonders just how long it'll be again until his search to feel, to know another, brings rise to the opportunity of escape.

He notices the change almost immediately and is relieved as it takes place, the emotions shutting off. They are followed shortly by empathy, understanding and acceptance. Bit by bit, his soul closes in on itself, not unlike the lights going off one by one. The outlying fringes stay open, the hints of all of them that he needs to get by day to day and remain functional enough to at least experience friendship and care for his existing relationships. It's so very dark now here, yet he finds the comfort he needs within. He's released this creature upon the world before, when he was much younger and did not fully realize he could control it nor that there would come the people who would erase it within him completely for spans of time. It feeds off his fears, it preys on others without any hesitation. At it's most powerful when the owner feels pain, it takes that anguish and devours the master. Turning those most terrible of feelings loose upon the innocent bystanders around. It wishes nothing more than to inflict hurt on the ones in his life that he invites in too shortly after the transgressions it perceives against it's master.

Who feels for such a person he wonders? Who cares for someone with the capacity to shut himself off completey from the world this easily? Does he attract damaged souls simply so he won't feel as bad if the beast gets loose on it's own, when his will is weakened by the idea of 'love'? He knows this to be false but in this darkness most needed right now, it's so very hard to find the truths within. He is a gentle soul, with so much caring and love to give that some times he feels like the dams inside will burst with the pressures they exceed on them. A faint hint of light shines through at this thought, he immediately blocks it out with a resolve like no other. He thinks back to a time not so far past and is thankful things happened as they did.

He had true interest in someone, he had not thought he'd feel that way at all so shortly after the final blow had been struck against him, yet he did. Fate seemed to have intervened and saved her from him in his weakened state. Perhaps things may have fallen into place and she had truly been a soul capable of silencing the sounds of darkness within him, he liked to think so. He also knows that it was for the best, for if he had been wrong and his judgement clouded by outside influence or an inner mistake, the beast could have surely gotten free without the owner noticing his agile and dark maneuverings.

STORY 334

He walks amongst the boxes we call homes, the cool winters breeze washing across his face. Thoughts of a chapter closing and another just beginning swirling around his head. The events most recent seeming to have no rhyme or reason yet he knows he shall find purpose once more. What is purpose outside of a basic financial need to keep a roof over your head and food on the table though? Does one actually need a purpose aside from that? Are we doomed to a need to label and define everything in life so that it seemingly creates meaning?

Is 'life' a purpose? A destination? Or is it better enjoyed when viewed as that series of moments, not unlike photographs littering an album? Is 'love' included in this mess of it all? What does love even mean to him? These are the thoughts that seem to pester him endlessly, that keep him awake at night and wake him far too early in the mornings. Unsure if he can even truly connect with another again, as that one moment seemingly washed away all the trust and understanding in another. This is the thought that is most recurring these days. That no matter how much energy he focuses on it, always seems to resurface the very next day like clockwork. He knows not what lays ahead and has chosen not to dwell in these places yet this question incessantly returns. Is the biggest tragedy of all in this the idea that one could become completely disconnected from themselves and others that they would not even bother to attempt to truly know another human being ever again?

Some youngsters speed by on the cold, white road, pulling himself from his mind briefly. They'll have to learn the dangers of that for themselves he mutters inside his head. Hopefully no-one will be hurt in that lesson passes through as an after thought. He checks his step meter on the phone and changes the song. It's found a sappy one and he really isn't in that place right now. A more positive and upbeat one comes on, he smiles to himself as he begins to sing it in his head as he resumes his wandering and musings.

His pondering to understand himself returns, this time focusing on the new interactions in his life. They've been mostly good at this point, a few hiccups and some pain he felt necessary to cause to keep people at bay. He realizes he can most certainly not invite anyone too far in at this point and yet he yearns for someone to see his true self, even though he himself has simply no clue what that is made up of this day. Has his desire to feel accepted by someone, anyone, skewed his vision slightly? He stays in this moment and ponders it more as he slowly and carefully treads down the icy sidewalk.

Have the recent meetings become some sort of twisted experiment for him to answer the one question with an answer that he may fear most? Is he willing to risk causing pain to another human being to basically fast track his own mind to a conclusion? Would that conclusion then be a reliable view of himself? He stops walking, lights a cigarette and inhales. This is one thing he knows he can't be doing anymore, his health rests firmly on the shoulders of his ability to quit this idiotic behaviour. He also knows that at this point he'll find or make any excuse not to stop, exhales and steps off the sidewalk into the intersection. The sun is beginning to set, casting some beautiful hues against the mostly overcast greys of the afternoon sky. He smiles at the simplicity in the fact that it's easy to recognize a sun as a need to our lives, yet we can barely distinguish the difference between a want and need for ourselves in all things heart/mind related.

A text brings him outside of himself, he pulls the phone from his pocket and glances down. It's her again, asking how his day has been going. He simply cannot stifle the smile that lands across his lips. He knows he likes this woman, she intrigues him, stimulates his mind and his passion. He feeds off her attention, his ego being stroked gently by it. Is he willing to risk losing that by standing in his own way? He knows he prefers to attempt to feel nothing at this point, wishes he could shut off completely but that's just not the case where she's involved.

Her kiss seems to hold a sweet promise behind it of just how much she has to offer herself, him, the world. He tries to compose and tell himself to act cool in this moment but also knows he's lying to himself and that he will reply immediately. He replies to her with a simple text telling her that it's been a good day and asking her how hers was. As soon as he hits send, he knows he's looking for the next text to read something along the lines of how she's been missing his embrace and kiss and can't wait to seem him again. That may not be what comes back across the screen but he can fantasize a bit, right?

STORY 335

She stands quietly, facing the steamed mirror caused by the warmth of the shower. Lifting a hand towel, she wipes at it, clearing enough to see herself. Some of the residue mist obscures part of her features but her eyes reflect clearly back at her. They hold a promise so sweet behind them, her truths bubbling beneath the surface. Sometimes she feels she's too young for them to have experienced so much. A life she's spent walking beside others and yet has anyone ever truly seen her? She's reached out once before, laid her soul bare in hopes that he would seek her spirit out and set it free from the bonds she herself has placed upon it.

The craving she feels inside, to find the one who will set her on fire from the inside out is almost overwhelming some days. Her only desire, to watch that phoenix that resides within fly free once more, like she fondly remembers it used to. Her eyes, those of a muse, catch her attention and pull her from her thoughts once more. They've known love, joy, compassion, empathy, understanding, trust, comfort and admiration....but most of all, they've known pain, frustration and disappointment. As life would have it, it's so much harder for the positive to cover the scar tissue of the negative than the other way around. No matter how she masks it, it is right there for the attentive to notice. Thankfully, many do not desire to see such things in people and most blindly walk past believing the smile upon her lips and within her eyes is all she knows.

She wonders if anyone will ever see her for all she is, all she has to offer and still welcome her in. Will someone accept her fully? Will they love her like no other? Although her perceived flaws and previous missteps weigh on her inside, it does not show in the manner in which she holds herself. She manages to cover that with a facade that pleases all social conventions. Will she herself even allow someone that far in, to seek her out? It's not even walls she has up that halts the pursuit of happiness. She likens it to a frozen river, laid out with thin ice and cracks. Herself on one side, those that dare on the other. They always seem to take the first step, driven by whatever reason they find in her. This is where the seemingly paralyzing fear sets in, she wants to take a step....desires it.

The road map of cracks across being previous inhibitions and pain. She knows them all too well, feels them reverberate through her as she reaches out with a foot and stops, leaves it dangling slightly above. Her hesitance and memories stop her once more and she withdraws from the bank again. She weeps gently within herself, the sorrow of the past breaching her today. The melancholy sets in as she knows she may hurt another with inability to at the very least take one step.

A single tear escapes her left eye in the mirror, she wipes it away quickly and comes out of herself. "Tomorrow" she whispers gently to herself. "Tomorrow, I will attempt again"

STORY 336

It's been a while now, more than a year, since i truly hear you speak. All that's left behind are memories, pictures and a voicemail that make me weak.

The worst part of it all is you never knew how it all made me feel. It could have been so simple, should have been so easy, to show the love to heal.

Two sisters wear their pain like a badge and show it when they cry. The brother, too stubborn, tries to stifle the emotion but knows he can't deny.

It feels like you should have taken better care and not be gone so soon. We're left missing time we could have shared, time under a bleeding moon.

Too late they come, my unspoken thoughts and love for you meaning zero. Never showed the admiration, love and respect you deserved, please know that you're my hero.

I need you now, more than ever in my life, amidst my pain and sorrow. I know you'd be right there for me, as you always were, if we had but one tomorrow.

STORY 337

Time passes on, the magnitude of the loss diminishing in the rearview mirror of life. Does time truly heal all wounds then? Lessen the perceived blows to ones soul? Or do the introspective paths one takes just show the events of the past for what they really were? Are tears really necessary? Or just formed by a blanket emotion shown for the 'idea of loss'? Is this what we grieve in matters o the heart, the concept of what we believe we should feel?

Perhaps I'm alone in all this, maybe i'm only one of few that questions whether or not his "feelings" do actually exist. This in turn lends an almost haunting undertone to my self reflection. Can one retreat so far into themselves that emotion and feelings become a charade without one noticing at all?

I saw her this day and although i felt a twinge of emotion rise, after 20 years, should i not hurt more? Losses spanning people and things and a life we had built, the concept of love and all its grandeur. The highs and lows, resembling the summits and the valleys, where has it all gone? Have i passed on beyond this place now? Is this perhaps why it's so hard to se even while the sun and my mind shed their light upon? Or did i pass on at some poin within it all, without even noticing? Replaced with some doppleganger whose sole purpose was to mimic my life and yet he fails simply because it cannot fathom how i believed i felt?

I feel again now, or do i? Am i myself or this soulless version of me? Since i am to find my own path in the darkness and i've misplaced my lantern, who shall do it for me? Are there even two versions of me? Shall i just split in two and allow one of me to find a light? Which surfaces now? The old me, the perceived false me? Or shall a new version of me appear miraculously to save the day? Armed with knowledge and revelation, shining his light toward the place i yearn to be.

When has one stayed in his own head too long? Is there an appropriate amount of time allowed by society and all their judgements? Do i care at all for those that wish to pass them upon me? I think not and yet, that will to be accepted drives me forward. Some say that being mired in too much thought can undo every truth around them, as they become lost to he paranoia within. Which is more blinding to ones soul? Too much thought? Not enough thought? Where has the middle ground gone? Why does it hide and not show itself to me?

Washing over me like the sea tortures the weak vessel, my musings easily capable of drowning me in their wake. We seek the things most easily attainable in life and yet pass over the same desire when it comes to truly finding oneself. Why is this? Are we afraid of the things we may find buried so deep within? Is it simply a matter of just accepting things as they are? It's so very simple to say things will work out as the universe intends and resign ourselves to waiting to find out where that seemingly preordained path leads. Yet, is it not our right to question it all? Is this simply not the idea of free will and mind? To question what we learn or are told or are brainwashed and programmed to believe.

The rambling ons inside can be silenced, in moments of belief in our views, expressions and ideas. True clarity of mind seems to be a lie? Again, there's a good chance that could be me alone? Are these constant battles waging inside just the two sides of my brain trying to function at once? My brain versus my heart? Or deeper yet, my soul versus my spirit?

I've become sidetracked in my own thoughts, as i am prone to do. If one could say "did you love this person, or just love the idea of loving them?'", then is it not right we question our very own ability to feel? Or do we just 'feel' because that is what we're supposed to do? What we've been led to believe we do as humans. If humanity can be faked, a concept we've been bred in to, what else lays ahead for us?

STORY 338

He stood close, gazing into the pools of promise she calls her eyes. Becoming lost within them as the world slowly slips away behind him. She knows not what he seeks inside, struggles to comprehend it all. Their lips resting against each other, slightly parted and exhausted from the kiss they've just shared. The breath escaping them in quick but deep sighs, falling like a cascading waterfall across their skin. The sweet caress of it all makes her feel alive and safe.

She retreats within herself just ever so slightly, unsure of just how he seems to see inside her soul so effortlessly. The past experience of pain rushes forward to reinforce the outer wall of her will as she feels herself begin to let go. Just as soon as she believes she'll be safe from him gaining more insight into her fears, dreams and desires, he reaches up and brushes her cheek lightly. She feels the butterflies rise inside her once more. She knows this touch, yearns for it. It is the touch of acknowledgement, familiarity, acceptance and trust.

He glides his thumb across her top lip and then downwards as his fingers hold her chin. He tugs gently at her bottom lip and pulls them apart even further. His lips touch her anew and in this moment the feelings begin to wash over her once more, easing her back into the place she feels safe and vulnerable all at once.

A realization comes forth as she melts into his embrace, strikes squarely in her mind. She is the muse to his words, to his soul and he craves her kiss more than he craves the breath in his lungs. She lets go completely and as the dam of her spirit and soul bursts at the seams, she offers herself up fully to him and the night.

STORY 339

It could have been any day
Like many others before
Yet the window she chose
To look out of, and beyond
Was not the one framed
By others intent and words
This one she had crafted
Unknowingly but with care
From a place of peace
That lay, somewhere deep
Finally, she had never felt
So beautifully full, wrapped tightly
In the fabric of herself
In a manner of a world
Newly found, presenting

To order more copies of this book, find books by
other Canadian authors, or make inquiries about
publishing your own book, contact PageMaster at:

PageMaster Publication Services Inc.
11340-120 Street, Edmonton, AB T5G 0W5
books@pagemaster.ca
780-425-9303

catalogue and e-commerce store
PageMasterPublishing.ca/Shop

www.ingramcontent.com/pod-product-compliance
Lightning Source LLC
Chambersburg PA
CBHW062155080426
42734CB00010B/1692